TECHNIQUES OF PROFITABILITY ANALYSIS

By SAM R. GOODMAN,
The Nestlé Company, Inc.

"Finance, as a discipline, has often carried with it the connotation of being stodgy. This book attempts to overcome that inference by introducing creative and innovative applications which integrate finance with the functional areas of marketing, manufacturing, and administration."
—from the Preface

Bridging the gap between theory and practice, *Techniques of Profitability Analysis* presents a businessman's approach to understanding profitability decisions. Written in clear, precise terms, it provides insight into the application of existing and new analytical techniques and their use in marketing and financial decision-making.

Including material not available in any other book, *Techniques of Profitability Analysis* contains discussions of

- the complex theory and applications of the return on investment concept emphasizing rarely used approaches to marketing situations.
- bringing together the considerations involved in determining acquisition policy, including methods of determining purchase price of an acquisition.
- the application of relevant costing to marketing applications.
- integrating marketing and financial planning through the use of product life cycles.

Techniques of Profitability Analysis is directed primarily at corporate executives who are interested in understanding the ramifications of finance in the functional areas of marketing, manufacturing, and administration. It is also valuable for financial specialists interested in innovative techniques in their own area and creative approaches to applying their functions.

TECHNIQUES OF

TABILITY ANALYSIS

ABOUT THE AUTHOR

SAM R. GOODMAN is Controller for The Nestlé Company. President of the Financial Executives Institute in Westchester, Dr. Goodman is the author of *Marketing Decision Techniques — An Innovative Approach Through Marketing Controllership* and *The Marketing Controller Concept*, both published in 1970.

Techniques of

PROFITABILITY ANALYSIS

SAM R. GOODMAN, Ph.D.
Controller, The Nestle Company, Inc.

WILEY-INTERSCIENCE

a Division of John Wiley & Sons

NEW YORK · LONDON · SYDNEY · TORONTO

Library of Congress Catalogue Card Number: 74-109427

SBN 471 31385 8

Printed in the United States of America

10 9 8 7 6 5 4 3 2 1

Preface

Many current books on finance, unfortunately, fall into one of two categories, being either textbooks or general-purpose informational literature. I have long felt that there is a need for some type of work that can bridge the gap between theory and practice. The intent of this book is that it not be considered a textbook. It is primarily aimed at the business executive who is interested in understanding the ramifications of finance in the functional areas of marketing, manufacturing, and administration.

Finance, as a discipline, has often carried with it the connotation of being stodgy. This book attempts to overcome that inference by introducing creative and innovative applications which integrate finance with the functional areas mentioned above. For example, the entire application of product life cycle theory and its transition to practical reality is, to the best of my knowledge, completely new. Furthermore, the application of relevant costing concepts is creative in that it leans away from the sparse textbook approaches to the subject.

It would be easy in this type of book to explain the topics in so much detail as to triple the book's size. I prefer to assume degrees of native intelligence on the part of the reader which will permit him to absorb the contents of this book without explaining them to death. In short, the approach in this book is to talk *to* people, not down *at* them. I, therefore, ask any readers puzzled by this approach to excuse my brevity.

SAM R. GOODMAN

November 1969
White Plains, New York

Contents

Incentive Planning • Qualitative Factors •
Quantitative Factors • Achievement of Size
Mixes • Sequential Steps for Solution • A
Simple Short Form Plan • Summary

List of Tables

List of Exhibits

TECHNIQUES OF
PROFITABILITY ANALYSIS

CHAPTER 1

The Marketing Controller—
Key to Increased
Profitability

One of the most fundamental teachings directed at students in the colleges and universities is that in order to define a problem, the students must first define its terms. In the academic sense, this is the proper way to attack a problem that involves logic and the need to make a decision; business, however, has frequently given short shrift to this approach for its problem solving. As a result, business has frequently found itself spinning its wheels because of its impatience at acknowledging the importance of defining its components.

The marketing controller concept is the by-product of a broad definition of marketing and finance, a definition which has been sorely lacking in industry.

WHAT IS THE CONCEPT?

The marketing controller concept is a *new* proposal designed to assist the marketing function in its planning and control. The roots of the concept derive from the quantitative expertise contained in the financial function, but its ramifications will extend its applications far beyond that for which the concept was originally intended. The proposal envisions the creation of a new corporate position, that of a marketing controller. The primary responsibility of this important new position will be to plan and control for the marketing function and to utilize free form in assisting the decision processes that have a quantitative base.

As decision-making becomes more complex and an increasing number of variables need consideration in the course of making a decision, it has become apparent that assistance requires far more than the establishment of a mere management information system. It requires an individual who is quantitatively trained, knowledgeable in the scope of the total corporate entity, who speaks the language of many disciplines. Initially, the marketing controller concept was just that, a proposal. Now that it is receiving broad exposure in corporate life and media channels, it is rapidly becoming a reality.

An evolutionary trend in that direction is the current development of appointing financially oriented individuals to the post of *advertising controller*. Large, sophisticated companies, such as General Foods, duPont, Johnson & Johnson, Trans World Airlines, and American Cyanamid, have all instituted financial control positions which directly oversee advertising and, in some selected cases, merchandising policies. The major functions of these individuals are to verify advertising bills, ensure the optimization of agency rates, negotiate agency contracts, and perform an audit function regarding the client's agency and certain of their suppliers.

THE NEED FOR A MARKETING CONTROLLER

These positions are evolving because it has become apparent that financial and control aspects of marketing are important to the success and efficiency of marketing programs. Current marketing practice is holding the marketing man increasingly responsible for profits, expressed in terms of return on investment, cost effectiveness, and profitability concepts. This new way of doing business has created problems because the present organizational functions are not ready or willing to meet the needs of these new evaluative procedures.

---

* The ideas expressed in this chapter are based on a work written by the author entitled *"Marketing Decision Techniques: An Innovative Approach Through Marketing Controllership* (The Management Center of Cambridge, 1970) where the results of the independent research mentioned in this chapter are discussed.

Finance, as a discipline, has become a very muddled area into which new techniques have been injected and into which the intercession of other disciplines is gradually forcing the financial officer into a defensive posture. It is becoming increasingly necessary for financial officers to be much better trained and more technically informed than ever, in order to contribute in this broadening base of what was a fairly well defined field. The evolution of sophistication in business practice and organization, as well as the emergence of data processing equipment and the changing nature of the marketing system, have created profound changes in an area which has heretofore been, in a relative sense, secure in the knowledge of its responsibilities and work roles. The function of controllership in particular, has suffered from a constriction of outlook as a result of the rigid conventions that usually define its duties. The Financial Executives Institute, for example, defined the function of controllership into these seven parts:

1. *Planning for control:* to establish, coordinate, and administer, as an integral part of management, an adequate plan for the control of operations.

2. *Reporting and interpreting:* to compare performance with operating plans and standards, and to report and interpret the results of operations to all levels of management and to the owners of the business.

3. *Evaluating and consulting:* to consult with all segments of management responsible for policy or action concerning any phase of the operation of the business as it relates to the attainment of objectives and the effectiveness of policies, organization structure, and procedures.

4. *Tax administration:* to establish and administer tax policies and procedures.

5. *Government reporting:* to supervise or coordinate the preparation of reports to government agencies.

6. *Protection of assets:* to assure protection for the assets of the business through internal control and internal auditing.

7. *Economic appraisal:* To continuously appraise economic and social forces and government influences, and to interpret their effect upon the business.

A recent revision to the listing by the Financial Executives Institute has given recognition to the shortcomings of the definition by including in the list the responsible assignments in the area of Management Information Systems.

Current controllership practice is being constricted by the above definitions. It is apparent that the principal orientation of the function in practice today is toward *reporting what has happened yesterday.* Its weakness is its inability to assist in *determining the probabilities of what will happen tomorrow.* In a speech a year ago, Keith Buckland commented on this when he said, "Many times it is difficult to distinguish what is financial and what is not financial in a company's affairs; very often its problems fall into the limbo between jurisdictions; other departments are only too happy to let the finance officer solve them." [1]

Earlier studies such as *Financial Management of the Marketing Function,*[2] sought to define controllership as it relates particularly to the functions of planning and control for marketing. For reasons perhaps best known to marketing management itself, the criticisms and constructive suggestions raised in that work have largely been ignored in practice to the present day. It is the suggestion of this research that an additional delineation of responsibility be added to the definition of controllership:

> *Utilization of creativity:* to establish alternative reporting methods designed to measure the effectiveness of performance responsibility under the marketing concept by measuring the fiscal implications of media and promotion policy and profit responsibility under the product manager system.

Changes in the field of accounting and marketing in the last two decades have created profound conceptual problems for the two professions and it is somewhat surprising that, in that interim, the professions have not conceived of an amalgamation of part of their common functions. Each is vitally concerned with profitability and with responsibility.

THE RELUCTANT CONTROLLER

Michael Schiff [3] once noted that accounting departments have never fully comprehended the marketing task and still retain the ancient notion that marketing is nothing but selling. Accounting has been traditionally oriented towards manufacturing and the techniques enabling the accountant to analyze cost systems. Now, however, new concepts in marketing planning and management are emerging which give eminence to decision-making techniques and it is forcing the entire field of management accounting

---

[1] A. Keith Buckland "Where Are We Going in Financial Management," *Financial Executive,* May 1967, Vol. 35, No. 5.

[2] Michael Schiff and Martin Mellman, *Financial Management of the Marketing Function.* New York, Financial Executives Research Foundation, 1962.

[3] A Dialogue between Professors Jack and Michael Schiff, "The Role of Accounting in Marketing," *Sales Management,* December 3, 1965.

to sit up and take notice. There is a reasonable question that may be asked concerning the identity of the individual who is equipped to speak with excellence about such subjects as input-output, value analysis, new product venture analysis, and management information systems. These changes, which are in the nature of changes towards greater specialization, are rendering the formerly held conceptions of the conventional controller's position obsolete. It is extremely unfortunate that in the past controllers have traditionally shied away from participating in marketing activities. There are few individuals who have the degree of sophistication and breadth of exposure to overall corporate activity as has the controller. It was only recently that in remarks to a business magazine, Lynn Townsend[4] said, "no profession I know of is more important than financial management."

RESEARCH INTO THE MARKETING CONTROLLER CONCEPT

An attempt was made to learn something about contemporary financial and marketing relationships in selected, large consumer organizations. Through the cooperation of the Marketing Science Institute and the Financial Executives Institute, I conducted personal interviews with twenty of the largest, consumer-oriented companies in this country. These interviews took place with the senior executives of marketing and finance within each company. The basic premise of the research was to test the validity of the marketing controller concept and its ramifications. That research effort was an outgrowth of my conviction that four major changes in the working environment are affecting the efficiency of the marketing function.

1. The basic structure of marketing has become increasingly oriented towards quantitative methods and techniques of management sciences. The research effort probed into the awareness and need for the marketing controller concept and yielded information which was found highly usable in evaluating current corporate organizational structures and their ability to meet modern marketing requirements. At the heart of the inability of the marketing function to properly use management science and other quantitative techniques are the organizational deficiencies alluded to.

2. The time has arrived to change conventional segmenting of professions. Instead, individuals trained in both the accounting and marketing areas

---

[4] Remarks by Lynn Townsend, "How Chrysler Restyled Its Top," *Business Week*, December 10, 1966.

should be required to assist the marketing function. The study found that greater quantitative inputs have highlighted the imperfections in the reporting relationships between the disciplines and made mandatory a more precisely defined linkage between marketing management and its financial counterpart.

3. Current controllership practice emphasizes the reporting function to management, owners, government, and the specific control of most non-marketing expenditures. The study found that future requirements based on marketing needs will be oriented toward marketing decision-making and control, and the evaluation of marketing costs.

4. It is time for the next step in the evolution of the controller as a quantitative individual. The time is ripe for the natural development of the controller, following the birth of the field of accounting and tracing a course from functional bookkeeping and fractionalized manufacturing controllership. It is time for the controller to specialize in various decision-making areas, specifically marketing.

All of the companies (or divisions of companies) participating in the study had annual revenues which exceeded $30 million. The distribution of the companies seen is set forth in Table I below:

TABLE I   Distribution of Respondents by Size (Gross Sales Revenues)

Amount of Annual Revenue	Number of Firms
Over $1 billion	5
$500–$999.9 million	6
$100–$499.9 million	7
$ 50–$ 99.9 million	1
$ 25–$ 49.9 million	1
Total	20

Each of the *companies* would have qualified to be listed in the *Fortune 500*. The aggregate sales for all of the companies or divisions interviewed totaled $16 billion, approximately 5% of the value contained in the *Fortune* listing. The product lines and major industry classifications for the companies were quite diverse and were chosen specifically to be representative of the broad base consumer market.

To probe the potential need for a marketing controller, it was necessary for the research to inquire into the following:

(a) The role of current controller practice in decision-making.

(b) Adequacy of organization and responsibility assignments within the companies and the weaknesses in marketing decision data input.

(c) The adequacy of financial analysis techniques for marketing and the involvement of personnel in data processing in marketing decisions.

On the basis of the replies given to the encompassing nature of the items under consideration, it is possible to make recommendations for implementing the marketing controller concept through the use of the establishment of a position guide and a discussion of the problems and possible solutions raised by the subject of the research.

CURRENT CONTROLLER PRACTICE IN DECISION-MAKING

One of the more interesting avenues investigated in my research effort was the questioning of the respondents with regard to the participation of their controller in the decision-making process of marketing. Heads of the financial and marketing areas were specifically questioned about the following:

> Purchasing policy
> Pricing
> New product ventures
> Acquisitions
> Sales incentive planning

The respondents were asked to rate the type of role played by the controller as either "major" or "minor," indicating the degree of decision-making responsibility in each area. Thus, if in incentive planning the role of the controller is merely to record and compute, that role would be categorized as "minor." If, on the other hand, he assisted in creating and evaluating the plan, his role could be classified as "major."

Somewhat surprisingly, as witnessed by Table II, the controller's role is generally limited to an ex-post responsibility. Each of the areas in Table II has, within its parameters, a potential marketing decision.

It is apparent looking at the table, that the controller's role, save for new product and acquisition evaluation, is limited in most companies.

The investigation of the controller's role in the *purchasing area* showed that the companies which have in common the characteristics of sensitive raw material requirements and strong financial discipline, were the same companies which indicated that their controller plays a strong role in decision-making for that area. Purchasing was chosen as an area because of its potential impact on profit planning in consumer companies.

TABLE II   Controller Participation in Decisions, Number of Companies Replying

Type of Role	Purchasing	Pricing	New Products	Acquisitions	Sales Incentives
"Major"	6	7	14	12	5
"Minor"	14	13	6	8	15
Total	20	20	20	20	20

One company, a cosmetic and fragrance company which was saddled with a very poor system for analysis and control, recently began a drive to cut costs. To implement that drive, the general manager of the division and the controller decided that they would make decisions on the long-term impact of costs and inform the purchasing agent as to the specific prices they wished him to try to obtain. In another instance, a health aids company indicated that the controller informs the purchasing agent of his "to buy" situation in order to meet profit plan requirements. This function is part of that controller's job specification.

Among the companies which expressed the opinion that their controller's participation in the decision-making process for purchasing was "minor," the study found that there is a divergence of causes for that situation. One company "lives with any costs they can get." Consequently, all that the controller has to do is to apply a standard material cost; any purchasing differentials are thrown out in the form of variances. Another company said, "the controller has little voice other than that of internal control. He exists in a service capacity only and has virtually no voice in decisions." In practice, the personality of the man himself was one of the major factors which lay behind the magnitude of the controller's role in purchasing decisions. Generally speaking, the research indicated that it was the strong controller who assumed the major role in decision-making, whereas it was the passive individual who permitted himself to assume no more than an "attest" function.

The *pricing area* is particularly sensitive because it has traditionally been a prerogative of the marketing function. Contained within all profit plans are assumptions regarding pricing structures. Deviations from that plan could have serious implications on operating results and, in addition, pricing policy frequently lives in the habitat of the highest executive levels. Given these considerations, it would seem at first that a natural disciplinarian would be the controller, the man most familiar with the requirements of the profit plan. This presumption is not, in fact, validated by practice. Only seven companies indicated that their controllers play a major decision role in pricing policy. Among those companies, one which felt that it was the epitome of the marketing concept indicated that its controller established the selling prices for all products based on a full cost margin. That same company, in fact, issued no financial data to marketing personnel whatsoever.

A health aids company indicated that its controller plays an active role in pricing decisions as an active member of the division head's staff. He sits in on all matters pertaining to pricing decisions. He does not, though, exercise a veto power unless there are truly significant instances of mispricing. Similarly, a major food processor indicated that its controller plays a dual role in pricing. He employs markeing services analysts who participate fully in the decision-making process that leads to a price change. These analysts act as expert advisors to decentralized division managers. Once a price-change decision is made, the controller indicates his concurrence by signing the price-change authorization. Even though his formal authority is in the guise of an attest function, the participation by his analysts in the strategy leading to the price change indicates that he plays a "major" role in decision-making.

Actually, many companies reported that the controller signs authorization type documents, but this appears to be more of a notification device to him rather than a symbol of any decision authority. It is interesting to note that each of the seven companies which replied that their controllers play a "major" role in the pricing area are wedded to extremely aggressive marketing policies (four of the companies are in cosmetics) and intense price competition. Another food-processing company was almost vehement in its rationalization about why the controller plays a "minor" decision-making role in the pricing area:

The corporate controller does not have veto power in pricing decisions, although he is a party to it. A closer party to price change action is the division controller. Philosophically, a price change is not a purely financial or marketing decision. If a marketing manager cannot unilaterally make the decision himself, then in fairness, neither the corporate or division controller should have the power to veto such a decision. The basic role of the controller is to assess its financial logic. In these reviews, judgemental factors are opposed to functional reviews. In the final analysis, most of the onus for being a watchdog rests with the division controller.

The area of *new product ventures* proved to be subject to the greatest financial impact. Controllers participate in review meetings in many of the companies. These meetings are held once or twice each quarter and consider new product possibilities. As a participant in these meetings, the controller is part of a team which makes an assessment of the problem in terms of the product's potential contribution. Many of the companies indicated that they had formalized this task and created new products committees which exist to perform that function. An interesting remark in the study came from one of the companies regarding its controller's participation in new product ventures:

In the area of new product ventures, the controller plays a role in the costing of a product. There is a great deal of room for improvement in this particular area because not enough is being done in utilizing the available financial talent. The controller should be brought into this area in the conceptual stage so that he may express a reasoned perspective on whether a product should be developed any further than its idea development. We have some projects now in motion which I am certain should never have reached that stage.

It should almost be taken for granted that the area of *acquisition analysis* would be heavily controller-influenced. This was borne out by the research. With one exception, the replies were rather perfunctory but did emphasize the financial nature of acquisitions. This attitude is interesting because not one of the respondents thought of commenting on what may be the basic reasoning behind any acquisition—the marketing influence. Indeed, most later rationalized under probing that the core of the desire is most heavily weighted with marketing considerations.

Sales incentive plans and planning showed itself to be a weak area for controller participation. Actually, the area is a prime function for active participation in decision-making on the part of the controller. Sales incentive planning is a type of medieval fortress whose drawbridge is raised or lowered by the sales manager. In addition, most incentive plans revolve around volume awards. This quite often breeds a consciousness of sales into the selling force but not a consciousness of *how* products should be sold or in what *proportions* they should be sold. In the absence of this appreciation, the salesman is encouraged to sell what is easiest for him to sell, even though the product may be one of the least profitable items for the company.

Based on profitability concepts, it would be a relatively simple task for the controller to take the initiative and demonstrate the optimum sales mix to the sales manager. Nevertheless, in most companies, it was indicated that the controller assists the sales area in the computation and evaluation of the incentive plan. For the most part, he acts as a monitor; he estimates the cost of a particular plan and then tracks down the results against the estimate. In only one company did the controller have the temerity to propose a different type of plan, not based solely on pure volume attainment. The result was that it was rejected for being too radical.

In an uncomfortably large number of instances (56% of the opportunities to play a "major" role), the controller acts as an "attestor." He has minimal roles in purchasing, pricing, and sales incentive decisions, but somewhat stronger roles in new product and acquisition evaluations. The results suggest that a massive waste of talent is taking place in controllership practice in the industrial groups represented by the respondents. Certainly, there is fertile ground in the purchasing, pricing, and sales incentive area for aggressive, constructive penetration by the controller.

Thus, current practice presents something of an impasse between finance and marketing. My impression is that if finance did not fulfill marketing decision needs, then that area would seek assistance elsewhere, possibly to the exclusion of finance. This has the potential of very serious adverse consequences. If it is possible for finance to take the lead and train "two-headed" men who utilize creativity for marketing purposes, the problem should be ameliorated. Finance must also view the concept as one of mutual trust. Fears were expressed that an individual such as the marketing controller might set up his own hidden reserves. However, this fear can be assuaged by proper reporting techniques and close working relationships. In the final analysis, the reporting relationship of the marketing controller is immaterial if the man in the job is positioned in an atmosphere of mutual trust and goals.

THE INFLUENCE OF THE MARKETING CONCEPT ON CURRENT CONTROLLERSHIP PRACTICE

The current situation is almost certainly an outgrowth of the emergence of the marketing concept in the postwar period. In the mid-1950s, the term "marketing concept" was popularized as a result of its employment by the General Electric Company. The "in" word then became "consumer" and corporate organizations underwent changes that permitted responses to actions derived not from the producing companies, but from the consumer. During the period when this change in emphasis was taking place, many attempts were made to define marketing. One of the early attempts was made by the American Marketing Association. It took the form of a description characterizing marketing as "the performance of business activities that direct the flow of goods and services from producer to consumer or user." In the context of inhibiting an interdisciplinary approach to marketing and financial cooperation, the definition can be faulted on two counts. First, it appears to place a great deal of emphasis on the economics of the marketing function, while disregarding the organizational aspects of the function.

Second, there is an implied assumption in the definition that the goods already exist. In essence, this would appear to rule out research and development activities, for example, from being included in the definition.

In 1965 Remus Harris[5] defined marketing as "the total procedure of creating customers efficiently." He changed the perspective of marketing and recognized in his definition that the discipline encompasses far more than an implied distribution function. A year later, the finest of the postwar definitions of marketing was espoused by Clarence Eldridge[6] in his series of essays for the Association of National Advertisers. He characterized marketing as "ascertaining, creating and satisfying the wants of people; *and doing it at a profit*" (italics mine). The uniqueness of the definition is in its totality and the recognition of the profit motive in American marketing. It was precisely the lack of implied profit motive which has inhibited the development of the controller into a total marketing man, and it is in this spirit that the concept of the marketing controller was born.

As the marketing concept emerged, the accountants themselves began to look at their own profession and question their roles in the marketing sphere. Some published articles attempted to establish a link between the accounting and marketing sphere and expressed it in terms of an "outside looking-in" relationship, whereby the accountant probed marketing as a devil's advocate probes potential candidates for canonization. For example, the accountant in this type of role asked the sales manager pointed questions about his sales force. The questions embraced many areas; for example:

Do you need a sales force at all?
How do you design territories?
How many customers do you want?

In retrospect, this was an extremely poor approach to a relationship whose end purpose is to establish a working harmony between two separate disciplines. In that type of posture, it is difficult to see the accountant as anything but "an expert from out of town." In none of these articles was the thesis expanded to suggest that the accountant could just as well be inside, as well as outside, looking in.

In essence, marketing may be the motivation which provides for the continuity of all other corporate services. The conception of a functional

---

[5] Remus Harris, "New Product Marketing Instituted by Agency V.P.," *Advertising Age,* December 27, 1965.
[6] Clarence E. Eldridge, *The Management of the Marketing Function, Sixteen Essays.* New York, Association of National Advertisers, 1966.

organization can best be described as taking the form of a wheel in which marketing is placed at the center akin to a hub, while the ancillary services of administration, controller, purchasing, engineering, data processing, and distribution all rim the wheel. Spokes, or lines of communication, emanate from the marketing area to each of the services, while additional lines of communication are positioned between the services (see Fig. 1).

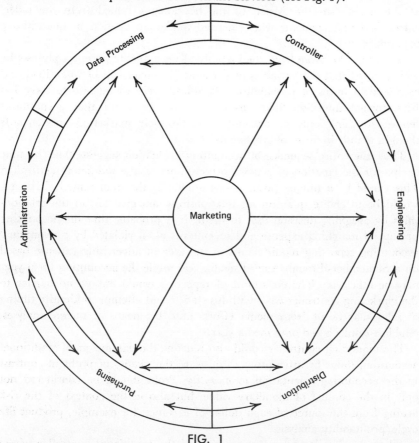

FIG. 1

This depiction attempts to more accurately portray the lines of communication which exist between marketing functions, the *raison d'être* for the business and its supporting services. In this regard, conventional line and staff organization charts have proven to be wholly deficient. As such, the conventional charts tend to give the reader a perspective of "to whom each box reports" or, in addition, whether one box is at a higher level than another box, inferring relative importance within the firm.

However, such depictions do not illustrate the nature of the continuous communications that are the heart of any decision-making process. The research data which were collated revealed that there were vast gaps in the network of relationships which are involved in quantitative marketing and financial decision-making. There was evidence of a great deal of hesitancy to use sophisticated decision techniques that could increase the efficiency of the decision-maker. Much of the hesitancy stemmed from the older, entrenched managements which needed modern education in quantitative techniques.

Hesitancy also arose from the inability of personnel to accept a philosophy which stated that the variables of consumer behavior can be quantified and expressed in terms of probabilities. Personnel were found also to have too little formal interdisciplinary exposure with the result that accountants tended to think only of accounting while their marketing counterparts thought mainly in terms of creative marketing.

Thus, the entire sequence of accounting evaluation suggests that the time is ripe for the creation of a new corporate entity, the *marketing controller*. This would be a unique position—as unique as the man himself. His task would be to create quantitative relationships and give life to the relationships by assigning decision uses to them. It is probable that the accounting precept of matching expense and revenues is often violated by conventional accounting reporting requirements in the area of advertising expense based on a September-through-August media year while the accounting fiscal year may be otherwise. The constraint of reporting would impose no barrier to the marketing controller who, with his staff, could attempt to identify timing of sales that result from media efforts and, by means of memo analyses, establish results based on a media year.

The marketing controller could also redefine the parameters of traditional accounting input by attempting to measure the *quality* of profit in contrast to the accounting orientation to *quantity*. Profit should be considered not only in the context of monetary value, but also in the context of the risk arising from the source of each dollar of earnings, for example, product life cycle/profitability analysis.

All of this is alien to the orientation of the traditional controller whose main responsibility is reporting. Certainly, without that orientation it is still conceivable, but improbable, that the conventional controller could accomplish much of the above.

THE MARKETING CONTROLLER— WHAT WOULD HE DO?

Each of the participants in the study was asked his reaction to the creation of a new corporate position, a "marketing controller." The marketing controller was described as a financially trained individual whose primary responsibility would be to provide the marketing area with decision-making assistance. He would have access to, and work closely with, the conventional controller whose main responsibility would be in reporting. The man would be placed within the marketing function in a decentralized organization and would be a corporate staff man in a centralized organization. Further, he would act as a filter for marketing with respect to all other quantitative input data.

Each participant was asked, "If a marketing controller's position were established in the functional marketing area, but relatively divorced from conventional accounting, how would his role be envisioned?" Most interestingly, *all 20 companies unanimously endorsed the concept with enthusiasm that ran the gamut from moderate to strong.*

When asked about reporting relationships for the marketing controller, the respondents replied as shown in Table III. By far, the greatest agree-

TABLE III   Primary Reporting Relationship for Marketing Controller— Replies

Report to	Number of Companies	Percentage of Total
Division marketing head	7	35
Corporate financial head	11	55
Other	2	10
Total	20	100

ment concerning a marketing controller's primary duties was that he should *maintain a record of adherence to profit plans.* One company, a large tobacco company, immediately concerned with diversifying into consumer areas, posited the man in their media area with a primary function of setting up statistical background for marketing decisions. Their marketing controller would, in effect, be a media controller. In carrying out his function, the marketing (media) controller would maintain a "track record for adherence to the profit plan" and play back to responsible parties the variations from the plan. The company's attitudes towards positing the man in the media area are shaped by their centralized financial and marketing operation and by their type of marketing policy (media are heavily emphasized).

Another consensus by the respondents was that the marketing controller should *advise on optimum timing for strategies.* One respondent, from a large drug and cosmetic firm, felt that the idea of a marketing controller had "great merit." He spoke positively of a marketing controller's position because "in these days of extreme competition, marketing management cannot afford to make decisions relative to pricing, volumes, and costs without knowing the profit impact of such decisions. They need a specialized financial advisor." In his estimation, the marketing controller would report to the marketing area and be considered a fully responsive member of the marketing team.

A large food and confectionary company felt that the marketing controller should be a "two-headed man" who could *understand and evaluate the effect on operations of marketing and financial requirements*. He would take the creative approach to these problems and concern himself mainly with the following:

1. Control of advertising and promotion.
2. Evaluation of promotion alternatives.
3. Analysis of the production costs of spot media commercials in order to evaluate customer and geographic profitability.

The company felt that, in a sense, the marketing controller should be its own division controller who, at times, becomes deeply involved in the assessment of marketing opportunities. It opined that the need is for future data and emphasis should be placed neither on historical data. nor on custodial reporting in conformance with traditional accounting methods although such men should work closely with the accounting controller.

Another company which had asserted that the concept is really not new but that nevertheless "it is an exciting idea," indicated that in the four months preceding the study, it had created the position of a division controller with this concept in mind. The responsibilities of their division controller, however, differ from the traditional and are very close to the spirit of the study. The men are mandated to *exercise free form in rendering assistance* and that is their only charge. They report directly to the division head and are not tied to the corporate controller, except for guidance. The men are freed from accounting and reporting rigidities and concentrate solely on decision-making assistance for marketing. Such an individual, they found, can communicate to marketing in its own language and breach the gulf in the company which exists between finance and marketing.

Almost all of the respondents indicated that one of the prime responsibilities of the marketing controller should be to educate the marketing area to the financial implications of decisions. A large health aids company indicated that this would be the man's primary responsibility. The company had found over a period of time that (a) by bringing in their sales forces and brand management from all over the country into a centralized location, and (b) by exposing them to the financial implications of their decisions, it reaped extremely large benefits in terms of increased efficiency and awareness of corporate considerations contained within its profit plan. As a result, this two-way communication has become a way of life with the company. The problem, however, is in finding a financially trained individual who can speak the marketing language. Too often the speakers or discussion leaders begin to lose the marketing audience through the use of jargon peculiar only to the financial area. The object is to find a "two-headed" individual who was born with one heritage but who has adopted a new native language.

The more aggressive companies, especially those in the cosmetics industry, indicated that one of the main advantages of such a corporate individual would be the assistance he would render in *evaluating the efficiencies of consumer promotions*. These companies realize that too often they had deluded themselves in rendering the criteria for promotional efficiency in terms of shares of market and volume gains. They conceded that the name of the game is still profit and that they are now beginning to see fallacies in the market share concept. The particular fallacy they refer to is the fact that the denominator is assumed to be an unchanging number. Additionally, they felt that volume gains are becoming decreasingly important criteria for efficiency since they have found, over periods of time, that such gains can be achieved easily if one is willing to purchase them.

An interesting variant on the consensus of the responsibilities for the marketing controller was contained in a reply from a package goods company which indicated that it is currently working toward that concept. The top executives viewed the position as concerning itself with "consumer values." Their marketing controller would be an individual who is capable of *rendering assistance to direct accounts* in order to help them automate purchases and optimize inventory levels. In this sense, he was to act as an "on-loan" management consultant.

The range of replies concerning the consensus of the marketing controller's primary duties itself is an indication of the needs which marketing feels should be fulfilled. It is in essence a measure of the shortcomings of the financial function. In summary, the following is the probable lineup of primary duties for the marketing controller:

- · · Maintain record of adherence to profit plans.
- · · Closely control media expense.
- · · Prepare brand manager's budgets.
- · · Advise on optimum timing for strategies.
- · · Measure the efficiency of promotions.
- · · Analyze media production costs.
- · · Evaluate customer and geographic profitability.
- · · Present sales-oriented financial reports.

• •Assist direct accounts to optimize purchasing and inventory policy.

• •Educate the marketing area to financial implications of decisions.

The means by which to incorporate these primary duties into a comprehensive job description for a marketing controller is discussed in the following section.

A JOB DESCRIPTION FOR THE MARKETING CONTROLLER

The following Position Guide for the marketing controller is based on the information derived from the study discussed earlier. In addition, it contains material which, in my view, should enhance the ability of marketing to utilize the marketing controller's quantitative acument.

The Marketing Controller—Position Guide

I. BASIC FUNCTION

The marketing controller administers the broad corporate financial/marketing planning function and its related programs as well as the preparation of such analyses as are requested. Attendant to the function will be a broad-based necessity to maintain liaison with the operating functions of the company with particular emphasis on providing assistance and advice to the marketing function regarding plans, budgets, and selected analyses.

II. SPECIFIC ACTIVITIES

A. *Planning and Analysis*

1. Guide the development of and recommend company-wide planning policies, programs, and procedures directed toward improving planning, scheduling, and control.
2. Advise and assist all marketing departments and divisions of the company, as requested, in the preparation of their departmental operating or capital improvement budgets.
3. Advise and assist in the preparation of all plant operating budgets, standard costs, and other cost information required for reporting and measuring production performance results.
4. Guide the consolidation of plans for capital expenditures as they affect marketing, profit and loss, and balance sheet statements,

and other budgets, for the company, including all plants and subsidiary companies, and prepare reports and comments presenting such budgets in accordance with approved procedures and schedules.

5. Guide preparation of estimates of profit and loss results from introduction of new or modified products.

6. Direct the monthly preparation of financial forecast of annual profits after receiving the advice and assistance of the controller, vice president—marketing division, vice president—purchasing, and vice president—administration division.

7. Participate with the vice president—marketing and marketing division managers in a minimum of monthly or more frequent reviews as required for revision of plans and forecasts.

8. Keep informed of new techniques in budgeting and forecasting and do whatever research is necessary in this field to develop data on new techniques.

9. Prescribe new and revised standard practice instructions regarding budgeting, profit forecasting, and cost accounting, in cooperation with the organization and systems department.

10. Work closely with advertising agency, both in developing plans and seeing that the creative and marketing brains of the agency are fully utilized at all times for the benefit of his assigned brands.

11. Direct a check and balance approach to review and evaluate progress; conduct a running audit of marketing plans and objectives versus actual performance, and recommend corrective action when and where necessary. Work closely with consumer products sales management and the field sales force to keep abreast of current sales and competitive activities in the market place; thus reacting in a timely manner to current competitive situations and opportunities.

12. Prepare economic evaluations and financial analysis to provide consistent division-wide approach.

B. *Reports on Operations and Performance*

1. Compare and evaluate actual profit and loss accounts against budgets for marketing division and submit the reports, together with appropriate analyses, to reporting heads prior to issuance.

2. Evaluate division results and make recommendations for profit improvement.

3. Guide the preparation and maintenance of sales and operating statistics and charts to provide necessary control information to be submitted to management.

4. Guide the issuance, analysis, and interpretation of all budget performance reports and assist managers at all levels in the development of remedial action to be taken to correct variances from plans.

5. Conduct regular and special assignments as directed, to include evaluation of the financial results of alternative actions.

6. Direct the design, form, and content of accounting reports to management, emanating from the marketing area.

C. *Cost Estimates and Evaluations*

1. Keep informed of sales and manufacturing plans and programs, and evaluate the implications of such on marketing costs. Close liaison should be maintained with the cost area.

2. Maintain continuous review and analysis of raw material market prices in order to evaluate their effect on marketing costs as they affect profit planning.

3. Be responsible for programs which will enable comparisons of projected selling prices in order to determine their relationship to factory and replacement costs based on current market prices for raw materials.

4. Review and analyze inventory positions relative to forecasted sales and production.

5. Prepare profitability estimates for new or modified products or processes with the assistance of the cost area.

6. Keep informed of the current market situation regarding raw material and company policy regarding raw material purchasing policy.

III. RELATIONSHIPS

A. *Controller*

1. The marketing controller is under the direction of and accountable to the controller, if centralized, to the division head, if decentralized.

2. The marketing controller prescribes to the supervisor of general accounting, the content and frequency of budget and performance information and assists the supervisor of general accounting as requested, in developing procedures for the preparation of required data, and ensures that the required cost information is supplied in a timely and accurate manner.

3. The marketing controller provides the controller with data needed to prepare the cash forecast and other basic reports.

B. *Vice President—Marketing*

1. The marketing controller will have a minimum of monthly or more frequent meetings as required with the vice president—marketing and the marketing division managers in order to obtain the necessary source data affecting budget and factory matters that involve the marketing division subject to the approval of the vice president—marketing and assist, as requested, in developing the procedures for the preparation of this information.

2. The marketing controller will report the effect on company profit and loss results of marketing and other divisions' actions and plans to the vice president—marketing and marketing division managers as information becomes available.

C. *Vice President—Administration*

1. The marketing controller will assist and receive advice from the vice president—administration relative to achieving corporate objectives for long-range planning. The marketing controller shall design and prepare a long-range planning format compatible with corporate requirements and objectives. Liaison will be maintained by means of periodic meetings with the vice president—administration and the controller.

D. *Vice President—Manufacturing*

1. The marketing controller will evaluate the financial impact on marketing operations resulting from capital programs undertaken by the manufacturing department. As data are developed, he shall report such results to the vice president—manufacturing as part of a continuous information plan system.

2. The marketing controller is responsible for the compilation and interpretation of the corporate capital program affecting marketing and shall maintain a close liaison with the manufacturing department.

E. *Vice President—Purchasing*

1. The marketing controller will have continual contact with the vice president—purchasing to keep informed of the current marketing situation regarding raw materials and company policy regarding raw material purchasing policy.

F. *Treasurer*

1. The marketing controller provides the treasurer with data needed to prepare the cash forecast and other basic reports.

G. *Chief Internal Auditor*

1. The marketing controller cooperates with the chief internal auditor to see that necessary information is furnished for approved internal audit programs.

H. *All Other Elements of the Company*

1. The marketing controller provides functional guidance and technical assistance to all company personnel regarding budgets, forecasting, and marketing analyses, including the publication and analysis of management reports. He makes full and effective use of staff services provided by other elements of the company and avoids duplication of staff and services in carrying out his responsibilities.

WILL IT WORK?

There is ample evidence contained in the results of the research that the implementation of the marketing concept will work. It is my personal belief though that the degree of success of the concept will depend heavily on the type of organization into which it is being injected. Because of the nature of fluid relationships which are contained more often in decentralized operations, it is apparent, based on intuitive logic and the consensus of replies from decentralized companies, that the concept is far more easily adaptable to such operations. At least three of the respondents indicated that they were either planning or had already started to implement such an idea.

In the one company which already began the implementation of such ideas, in the four months prior to the actual timing of the research, there was indication, based on conversations with the affected executives, that they were highly pleased with the start of the program and that it had created a climate of confidence in which, for the first time, individuals from diverse functional areas actually felt that they were all working for the same company.

Regardless of the implementation, the essence of the concept lies in the climate of permissiveness which will allow the quantitatively trained financial man, who has his heart in marketing and can speak the marketing language, to fully participate and lend his talents in an area from which he has hitherto been largely excluded.

CAN A MAN SERVE TWO MASTERS?

Over three-quarters of the respondents to the study indicated that their financial function was highly decentralized. Many of the companies, which reported that their financial operation was decentralized, indicated that their division controllers reported directly to the division head but still retained a "dotted line" relationship to the corporate controller. All indicated that this has proven to be a viable relationship, giving confirmation to the findings of the earlier Controllership Foundation Study[7] which concluded that the evidence "indicates that a division of formal authority is entirely workable." They further concluded that a man can serve two masters, provided that the two masters are not working at cross purposes. Because the marketing controller cannot work in a vacuum, he must depend on the conventional controller to supply him with the basic source material for his creative analysis. In this manner, he will probably have frequent contacts with both the division and corporate staff controller. It would be natural to anticipate early stages of envy or skepticism when the position is first initiated. However, logical reflections should dissipate this attitude quickly.

A CONTROLLER'S SPY?

One of the respondents in the study is now attempting to achieve a marketing controller concept. This company is in the process of centralizing conventional accounting and it intends to shape the job of its present division controllers away from the reporting aspect and more towards the creative decision-making area. The feeling here is that the marketing controller should report to the general manager of the division rather than to the corporate controller, since the function is decentralized. The respondent also felt this desirable because an onus would be placed on the man otherwise and, "I don't think marketing would tolerate a spy in its midst." That this point should be raised at all is indicative of the sensitivity existing which is a carryback from the earlier expressed attitude on the part of the financial profession towards marketing. It is little wonder now that the hangover from that attitude has become the sensitivity to the breaking down of little kingdoms of information.

Strangely, finance too is extremely sensitive in a jealous guarding of what it considered to be its original prerogative of the sole information-gathering

---

[7] *Centralization vs. Decentralization in Organizing the Controller's Department.* New York, Controllership Foundation, Inc., August 1954.

arm of the company. An extremely large, multibillion-dollar food processor indicated that it feared the marketing controller might have the ability to set up his own "hidden reserves" which would be shielded from the conventional accounting controller and thus result in manipulation of profitability statements. From a technical point of view, this is the type of problem which can be solved fairly easily through proper checks and balances in the record-keeping system. The problem that is more difficult to solve is the person-to-person communications relationship which may find two people in the same profession acting at cross purposes—witness the conventional and the marketing controller.

There is a well validated need for a marketing controller. One large drug and confectionery company indicated its dissatisfaction with conventional accounting procedures. The marketing manager of the consumer products division employs off-invoice allowances as a selling technique. Use of this device permits the customer to remit on a net basis after having taken credit for specified allowances for merchandise purchased. As such, it is part of the regular marketing mix. The use of the technique is controlled by the marketing manager. The amount to be issued to the customer in the form of a credit is controlled, as well as the dates during which the promotion is effective. Nevertheless, in the eyes of traditional accounting, and more importantly in the eyes of the Securities and Exchange Commission, such a promotion is a *de facto* price decline. Moreover, it must be reported as a deduction from sales proceeds.

The marketing manager desired to inform his sales force and his product managers of the magnitude of this type of selling expense. He asked the conventional accounting controller to have the product operating statements recast so that this expense would appear as a promotion expense in the general marketing category. His request was refused by the controller because it was contrary to SEC reporting requirements. Such an example of industrial practice makes only more imperative the need for a marketing controller who will have the knowledge and the ability to recast operations and operating results in the form of fiscal or *pro forma* statements.

DO WE ALREADY HAVE
MARKETING CONTROLLERS?

Some few companies do have individuals who have been vested with the title of a marketing controller. However, the concept of the position, as practiced by these companies, is quite different from the proposal outlined in this book. Many of the companies interviewed in the research, as noted earlier, felt that they had either just embarked or were about to embark on the creation of such a program. The marketing controller concept, as such, is in many ways a question of attitudes. It could very well be true that many practicing professionals in the financial area have already assumed many of the duties outlined.

What has been lacking, however, is the formal recognition of the implied responsibilities for the position and a recognition by both the marketing and the financial area that the decision-making needs in each discipline are quite specialized. Decision-making in marketing has the potential of becoming another Tower of Babel. In many areas, marketing is already receiving assistance from financial areas that are attempting to increase the efficiency of marketing decision-making. It is questionable, however, whether there is a sufficient appreciation of the different language of marketing on the part of their financial help. The financial orientation to marketing is in the form of control and Peter Drucker[8] perhaps said it best when he indicated that ". . . most, if not all executives, including most controllers themselves, would consider it a gross misuse and abuse of controllership were this 'controller' to use his 'control' to exercise 'control' in the business."

The Nestlé Company has taken a positive step in the direction of implementing the marketing controller concept. The company is highly centralized in all major areas with the exception of marketing which is organized in a divisional manner. The marketing divisions depend on the centralized corporate services for administrative purposes. The controllership function is included among the centralized operations servicing the marketing divisions. This takes the form of providing custodial accounting, financial planning, and cost estimating assistance.

In 1965, the financial operations of The Nestlé Company were reorganized so that a specific segment of that operation would be made available to the marketing function for marketing planning and control. Mature, quantitatively trained individuals, who were highly marketing oriented, were assigned to each of the six major marketing divisions. The object of this assignment was to enable the divisions to have the benefit of creativity in the use of financial and other quantitative advice affecting the profitability and strategic evaluation of marketing alternatives.

The specialists, called marketing service analysts, are divorced from any custodial accounting and profit planning functions and accept their assignments directly from the marketing head of each division. They report to the controller only for a review of progress on specific assignments and for the

---

[8] Peter Drucker, "Controls, Control and Management," in *Management Controls: New Directions in Basic Research,* Charles Bonini, Robert Jaedicke and Harvey Wagner, Eds. New York, McGraw-Hill, 1954.

more routine personnel evaluations. Aside from that reporting relationship, the analyst is, in effect, an internal, quantitative consultant. The area has proven to be a significant training ground for future managers within the company. The exposure to marketing, inventory control, production planning, and marketing research has proven to be of such value that there has been a complete turnover of the initial group of marketing services analysts. The initial group has all been placed in the above areas as operating personnel.

It is difficult to describe the specific assignments of these men, however, the nature of their assignments has encompassed such diverse problems as the following:

1. Evaluation of customer and geographic profitability.
2. Development of the profitability of roll-out patterns for new products.
3. Evaluation of the feasibility of new facilities for product production.
4. Evaluation of the implication on profitability of hypothetical commodity assumptions.
5. Assistance in developing meaningful, actionable management reports.

SUMMARY

It is apparent, based on the trends already in evidence and the replies to the research effort, that mature individuals are needed who are capable of providing financial and other quantitative assistance to the marketing areas. It would be an easy criticism to state that the accounting and control function is not a major problem in marketing and that it is relatively well handled in most companies. The evidence at hand, including the earlier Financial Executives Institute study, currently indicates that such is not the case, and the results of my own research and acquaintance with business practice in other companies, convinces me that the problems and issues raised in that earlier study are still largely unsolved. In all probability, the training program for the development of a marketing controller would take a couple of years to satisfactorily accomplish.

Obviously, such men are hard to come by. In the interim, however, the starting point might be intensive marketing training, orientation, assimilation, and exposure for select groups of bright, young individuals who are quantitatively trained in the broad financial area. It is probably easier to make a marketing man out of an individual who has received his basic quantitative training than it is to reverse that process. Bernard Baruch once said, "There is no secret to making money, if that's what you really want to do." In much the same vein, there is no secret to implementing the marketing controller concept, if this is truly what all parties want to do.

The foregoing discussion has demonstrated the wide-ranging views and existing duties of such an individual. Certain common threads run through all of the descriptive backgrounds for the position. The remainder of this book will show more concisely how a creative individual can assist the marketing function in making faster, more meaningful decisions.

Chapters 2 and 3 discuss the use of Relevant Costing in operating statements. This technique is most useful in assisting the decision maker to measure the efficiency of promotions, evaluate customer and geographic profitability, and optimize the timing of various marketing strategies. In addition, it is an excellent vehicle for keeping a record of variances from profit plans.

Chapters 4 and 5 break ground in the relatively untouched area of product life cycles. The creative financial man has a fine area for utilizing a new approach to marketing analysis in this field, for it is here that the marketing controller can begin to speak the language of the *quality* of profit as opposed to the custodial accounting view of measuring the *quantity* of profit.

Chapters 6 through 9 demonstrate a creative approach to the uses of Return on Investment. These approaches are directed mainly at the marketing and operational areas. It is here that the marketing controller can demonstrate the implicit truth that, for instance, the basic decision behind a prospective acquisition is in the nature of a marketing consideration. His efforts in analyzing such a prospect should be highly marketing-oriented. To be sure, many tax and equity considerations may be present at the root of the corporate marriage; however, a marketing rationale must also be present. There are few more promising areas for the quantitatively trained individual to look into than establishing the selling price for a product and evaluating the efficiency of a geographic selling area and of the sales force.

Chapter 10 discusses specific areas in which new life can be breathed into the traditional marketing enclaves of sales analysis and incentive plan construction. The discussion earlier revealed that the current controller practice virtually excludes financial participation. This is sad in view of the fact that wise decision logic, utilizing product mix, could contribute so much.

CHAPTER | 2

Using Relevant Costing to Determine Profitability

In this age of vocal dissent, it is surprising that this type of expression has not found its way into the more cloistered executive offices; today's business practices and techniques warrant such action.

"Profit" has become a badly used term. It no longer has a single, unifying definition and the fault probably lies in the myriad of end-uses of the concept as business has become more complex. These complexities culminated in the use of the marketing concept and the practice of so-called "management science" techniques. The term, "management science" now has generally come to mean such operational techniques as:

Linear or other mathematical programming
Critical path scheduling (Pert)
Queuing (waiting-line) models
Economic order size or other inventory models
Simulations
Factor analysis
Regression analysis
Statistical sampling

Each of the above techniques is specifically designed to define segments of decision sequences so that the executive can isolate the important areas, relative to the decision which needs to be made. In a somewhat similar vein, the marketing concept has attempted to isolate the responsibility for marketing decisions and profits. Specifically, it has given birth to the concept of a product manager and the popularity of a type of accounting called "responsibility accounting." This has helped to give us an appreciation of defining and planning for the variables which comprise the calculation of the number which is to become "profit." Despite the assistance given to the product manager through the utilization of "responsibility accounting" techniques, it is still often difficult for the performance of the product manager to be efficiently measured, because often the profit with which he is credited is not the profit which he can directly *control;* rather, it is often the profit which he can *influence.*

PROFIT VERSUS PROFITABILITY

When we discuss the distinction between profit and profitability, we enter into the area of debate between two separate disciplines. On the one hand are accountants, trained in summarizing what happened *yesterday,* who espouse traditional accounting reporting. Their professional, loyal opposition are the men representative of modern corporate finance.

To the former, profit is a residual. It is a static, historical term, more geared to a reporting function than to decision-making. Accounting techniques give the controller the means with which to influence the direction and magnitude of profit. One of the major arguments both for and against the concept of pooling of interest in mergers and acquisitions is just this point of the ability to affect reported profit.

In contrast, profitability connotes dynamism and is espoused by the champions of contribution techniques, such as direct costing. These techniques, which will be extensively treated, are especially useful in viewing isolated marketing and production problems. In the late 1950s and the early 1960s, the phrase "Profitability Accounting" became popular. In a recent book, Beyer gave this definition of the concept:

A single unified accounting structure should satisfy simultaneously the objectives of financial (or custodial) accounting and those of managerial accounting. The system is complex, involving the integration of all the modern, profit-oriented, accounting techniques into a single, *decision-impelling,* management information system.[9]

---

[9] Robert Beyer, *Profitability Accounting for Planning and Control.* New York, Ronald Press, 1966, p. 4.

The modern corporate finance man views the distinction between profit and profitability as a test of ownership. Profit is an owner-oriented concept and is tied into the ownership shares of national income and the provision of equity capital for business enterprises. In the total corporate sense, it is the measure of wealth maximization and the yardstick for distribution to enterprises and individuals of wealth that *will* be created.

Profitability, on the other hand, as a concept, is akin to levels of profit which lend themselves to the least number of alternative accounting techniques and satisfy the criteria that will measure the profit *directly attributable* to the existence of a product and identify marginal contributions. It is essentially an internal measure of new wealth creation. Thus, whereas the accounting concept of profit measures what has been accumulated, the analytical concept of profitability is concerned with future accumulations of wealth. The concept of variable profit which will be discussed in the remainder of this chapter is designed as the increment of profit which will accrue as a result of changes in volume. In one sense, it is very close to the economic concept of contribution margin. The difference between contribution margin and variable profit often lies in the inclusion of nonmanufacturing expenses which have a variable behavior pattern.

The current views of profit are deficient for decision-making purposes because of the ease by which such numbers can be manipulated and, in using this choice of semantic description, I am not implying immoral or illegal manipulation. Rather, I am attempting to rationalize the relative freedom given the controller, within bounds of consistency, under the so-called "generally accepted accounting principles." The use of this freedom is compounded by the different uses of profit in corporate operations. It may be a vehicle for pricing purposes, for ownership reporting, for management analysis, or for tax reporting. Consider further, then, that we are confronted with, in effect, a group of statistical variables which can further lead to a pairing-off of considerations; for example, reporting to the government for cost-plus pricing purposes. The same set of numbers can yield a different answer depending upon to whom the profit is being reported. Profits reported to stockholders may be based upon straight-line depreciation for assets; the same numbers, reported to the government on an accelerated basis and reconciled on Schedule M of tax returns, yield a different result. Under proposed requirements of the Securities and Exchange Commission there may be yet even more variations of reported profit, probably in the form of contribution levels for division or product lines. The following is only a partial listing of these techniques and their ramifications.

• • *Straight-Line versus Accelerated Depreciation.* Expenses for depreciation are a taxable deduction on a profit and loss statement; the greater the expenses, the lower the reported profit, however; that large expense also reduced *cash* payments for taxes because the profits are reduced. Conversely, straight-line depreciation charges off the cost of an asset over an even pro-rata rate for the same time period, tending to reduce expenses and thereby increasing reported profit, *but* also *increasing* cash payments for taxes.

• • *Capitalization versus Expensing Capital Items.* There are many options that exist in accounting for capital items. One of these is the judgement factor involved in classifying work as capital or expense. The choice can have a profound effect on profit because pure capital items are assets whose costs must be amortized over the useful life of the asset or groups of assets. Expenses, on the other hand, are deducted *in toto* in the year incurred. Thus, both the magnitude and timing of the expense are critical to profit and are directly influenced by the decision. Judgement becomes important when projects have elements of both capital and expense contained within. Conceptually, capitalizing is involved when the process will create or add to the useful life of an item. When a new plant is constructed adjoining an existing one and walls in between must be demolished, the roof strengthened, and new piping installed, it is questionable as to the status of some of these items. A similar case can be made for certain start-up costs for the new plant. Is the shaking-out, the perfection process, integrally related to the status of useful life of the project? The answer is judgemental.

• • *FIFO versus LIFO.* This technique of valuation influences the cost of the goods that are manufactured and then sold and, further, since the variable in each technique is the valuation of the final inventory, the choice of each technique affects profit. Choosing LIFO (last-in, first-out) in times of rising raw material prices affects valuations by placing the highest priced materials (last-in) into production and clearing them out through sales (first-out). The inventory that is left contains the lower cost materials bought at the beginning of the price rise cycle. Since the later, higher cost items have already been sold, profits, and most importantly, cash payments for taxes as a result, are reduced. Strategically, the conservation of cash in times of rising prices is quite consonant with sound business judgement. It is not all one-sided though, because in times of falling prices, the reverse takes place and a business can find itself paying high taxes to the government when it needs cash most to take advantage of opportunity purchases.

FIFO takes the opposite tack. The materials purchased first are assumed to be immediately consumed and the inventory valuations left are at the most recently purchased values. In times of rising prices, this produces higher profits since the lower cost materials (first-in) were consumed and sold. One advantage, however, of FIFO (over LIFO), is the ability of the technique to produce "inventory profits" in times of rising prices if the merchandise in question is priced based on current cost trends. This occurs when anticipatory price increases are effected covering merchandise that will not be sold until a later date. FIFO, however, can be a two-edged sword in periods of price declines. Lower profits will be reported under FIFO during such times because as prices gradually fall, the end of the period lowest prices will be valued into inventories as a result of the use in production of the initially bought, higher-priced materials.

• •*Accounting for the Investment Credit.* The movie, "The Odd Couple," paired people of diverse philosophies in a situation where each had a common interest. Accounting infighting can accomplish the same thing. A stirring occurred recently which brought together two strange bedfellows arguing for a cause of common interest. The majority of practicing professional C.P.A.'s and the Treasury Department took issue with pronouncements of the American Institute of Certified Public Accountants for their advocacy of accounting for the Investment Credit by amortizing it over the life of the asset which created the credit. The credit is just that—it's not cash but an allowance which reduces taxes payable. Amortizing it over a period has the effect of mitigating the tax reduction. In opposition, the "odd couple" contends that it was clearly the intent of Congress to offer immediate and substantial incentives to spur major impact on profits because operating profits are not affected by the technique. Taxes are simply reduced, thus dramatically increasing earnings *after* taxes (and more importantly, cash payments), the basis for "earnings per share."

The list is fragmentary but an inescapable question manifests itself. Is it any wonder that a decision based upon a number called "profit" is shaky? The far more preferable concept to be used for decision-making is "profitability," alluded to earlier, but which will now be discussed in depth. Profitability, in its *simplest* terms, is most *like a level of worth*. Profit is static and conventional; profitability, dynamic and innovative.

USABLE PROFITABILITY CONCEPTS IN MODERN MARKETING

With the above discussion as a background, we will proceed to develop profitability concepts usable to the management accountant. This type of concept should be a level of profit which can be employed to evaluate, plan, and decide on alternative strategies. Moreover, it must be compatible with the "new marketing concept."

In order to develop the profitability concept, a two-step procedure will be necessary to bypass conventional accounting methods such as absorption and direct costing. Essentially we are concerned with *future* costs which will change. This is very much like taking costs and prices and throwing them up into the air. Out of the mound that settles, only those items attributable to the decision at hand will be picked up because they alone are the relevant considerations. In a given marketing situation, such costs might be of a type associated with short-term marketing and production activity such as promotions, advertising and display allowances, or incremental factory overhead.

• • *Relevant Costing.* In a given decision situation dealing with a problem not yet in existence, sunk costs—those which already exist—cannot affect the outcome of the decision. Conversely, should the problem never come into existence, those costs will go on anyway because they already are in existence. I do not question whether sunk costs are important; they are. They are real, they cost money, and they must be recovered. The key in profitability and relevant costs is whether sunk costs would exist irrespective of our decision. If they do, then, by inference, they cannot affect the decision.

To meet the initial decision requirements of business, standard costing on an absorption basis was developed. Absorption costing is a production/volume-oriented approach designed to highlight the degree to which product and sunk costs have been applied to production. For example, when production is higher than anticipated, costs are "over-absorbed" which results in turn in higher inventory values and favorable profit variances. Underplanned production produces the reverse.

• • *Direct Costing.* Direct costing or contribution accounting is likewise production/volume-oriented because it seeks to assign variable manufacturing costs to a product. Even so, direct costing is really a misnomer. It does not account for all costs directly attributable to the existence of a product, a project, or an hypothesis, or things of this kind. What of direct advertising and promotion and incremental factory overhead? A better name for direct costing is variable manufacturing costing because it is at that level that the analysis stops. Certainly the costs may not all be direct and, moreover, the system only accounts for manufacturing costs. It fails to recognize that once a product is manufactured, it still must be marketed.

Stopping at that level is untenable for a marketing-oriented company. The essence of variable costing (direct costing) is that fixed overhead costs (sunk costs) such as selling and administrative costs (including marketing media and promotions) are too remotely related to the product to be attached to its cost. This is nonsense to the modern marketing executive who places reliance on the goals of volume attainment and allocation of all costs and the magical significance of something called "gross profit."

SOLVING MARKETING-ORIENTED PROBLEMS WITH RELEVANT COSTING

What are the solutions to the myriad of marketing-oriented problems: cost-volume-price relationships, product mix, size mix, pricing, distribution methods, media/promotion mixes, product manager profit responsibility, ROI for products, group of products, divisions?

Relevant costing is much more of a solution than direct costing because it attempts to infer precision and relevancy to the economic existence of the item being measured. Any cost is relevant if it generates a negative answer to a question such as: "If we did not do this (make the product, build the factory, add a flavor, a size, etc.), would be still have the cost?" Plainly, we are dealing here with an economic concept of incremental costs.

ABSORPTION COSTING CAN BE MISLEADING

Exhibit 1 shows a conventional profit and loss statement. This statement is currently in use by a major company whose sales easily exceed $1 billion. It is quite satisfactory as a vehicle for reporting aggregate results on a company, division, or product basis. Its useability, however, is precisely the very nature of its *reporting* orientation. The defect in this type of statement is that it is not geared to bring together information which is critical in a decision sense. The category "gross profit" is a profit level which includes the effects of factory period costs which are included in "cost of goods sold." It immediately renders this statement useless for ascertaining marginal manufacturing costs. Period factory costs (such as supervisory labor), by their very nature are costs which are more likely to vary over a period of time than with a unit of production. They also have a tendency to vary in step patterns, keying themselves in with changes in manufacturing capacity.

As an example, if a facility has period manufacturing costs of $1 million and is currently making 10,000 units of a product, it is quite conceivable that if unit production were increased to 12,000 units, the $1 million of period costs would not be affected. Only those costs would be affected which vary directly with production such as, direct labor, direct material, and any *incremental* overhead such as certain utilities. However, it may be that if production were increased to 15,000 units, the optimum capacity for operations at that level of period costs could be reached and new packing lines with their attendant supervisory labor may have to be installed. Only then does the level of period costs change.

Given the above, it may be easier to understand why one cannot immediately answer a question which, in its simplest form, may ask, "If I increase my production (sales) of Product A from 10,000 units to 11,000 units, what will be the effect on gross profit?" Sunk costs were referred to earlier. Exhibit 1 is a prime example of an area where sunk costs are melded into cost of goods sold; an area which, for decision purposes, should include only direct costs, both variable and nonvariable.

Below the gross profit level, marketing and distribution expenses are properly delineated. However, there is no attempt made to segregate any of these costs in terms of those which are directly attributable to the existence of the product or the division in whose statement they are contained, nor is there any attempt made to classify any one of those expenses which are variable with units of sale. As an example, media expense can be an amalgam

EXHIBIT 1   Conventional Profit and Loss Statement

Proceeds from sales			$250.0
Cost of goods sold			170.0
Gross profit			$ 80.0
Operating expenses			
Advertising—media		$12.0	
Deals		10.0	
Selling			
Field	$ 3.0		
Administration and product management	1.0		
Market research	0.5		
Total selling	$ 4.5	4.5	
Total marketing expense			26.5
Merchandising profit			$ 53.5
Research		$ 3.0	
General and administrative		12 5	15.5
Profits before taxes			$ 38.0

of institutional advertising, product *line* advertising, or individual product advertising. For decision-making purposes, only that media expense attributable to the existence of a specific product should be charged against the product on its operating statement. To do otherwise again masks the decision ability of the reader to isolate the impact of a product.

Further, as an example, let us assume that Product A, a candy bar, is one of twenty candy bars manufactured by the Ultra Chocolate Company. In its efforts to establish the Ultra identity in the minds of the consumer, Ultra has created a logo of a split cocoa bean, oozing rich, brown chocolate. There are times when the Ultra Company advertises only the logo and there are also times when the company advertises its product lines of candy bars. In addition, there are occasional spot television ads for Product A. From a decision point of view, only the spot television ads for Product A are directly traceable to Product A. To allocate portions of the advertising for product lines or the cost of the logo to Product A only confuses the issue. In actuality, the advertising for product lines is attributable to the existence of the retail chocolate division and is properly a *division* expense. Similarly, the logo is virtually a corporate expense, a charge related to the efforts of the corporation to establish a chocolate identity.

The expense called *deals* is a synonym for promotional efforts. Deals may take many varieties or forms. In some instances, they may take the guise of an off-invoice promotion which many companies choose to consider as a reduction of sales rather than a marketing expense. The motive behind that action is usually that it is in conformity with requirements of the Securities and Exchange Commission which dictates that *de facto* price declines are shown as a net of sales. In reality though, off-invoice promotions are controllable marketing expenses and if the reporting nature of the operating statement is distinguished from its decision-making function, off-invoice deals should properly be charged as an expense. Moreover, it is a *variable* expense since it is incurred on a per case basis.

Other types of promotions, however, may not be variable, such as advertising and display contracts or other forms of cooperative merchandising agreements. Therefore, in Exhibit 1, it is readily apparent that no effort is made to distinguish between those promotions which vary with volume or those which do not.

Selling expense, with the exception of commission salesmen, is essentially a period expense. The question must be asked that if the product did not exist, would the same amount of selling expense, excluding commissions, also exist? If the answer is yes, then that amount should not appear on a decision statement since it is irrelevant to the existence of the product.

Furthermore, in the same statement, research and general and administrative expenses are grouped without specifically answering the question as to what increment of these expenses exist because a product exists. If they are truly a staff function, there would be little decision benefit to allocating a portion of the staff function to the product.

Lastly, the lowest profit level on this statement, "profit before taxes," implies that a product pays taxes. I submit that this is a specious point of logic and that this level of profit only follows because of the attempt to apply so many irrelevant expenses to the product.

THE FAILURE OF DIRECT COSTING AS A MARKETING TOOL

Exhibit 1 is a statement which might be produced by a firm utilizing full absorption costing. A more sophisticated variant of Exhibit 1 is to be found in Exhibit 2 which shows a conventional direct costing statement emphasizing the contribution margin approach. Notice that this too is deficient because it does not truly permit marginal analysis below the manufacturing contribution level. Implicit in this statement is the reinforcement of a point made earlier about the manufacturing orientation of the accounting systems.

EXHIBIT 2   Example of a Conventional Direct Costing Statement

Sales		$250.0
Variable cost of sales		
Variable manufacturing costs—less ending inventory		140.0
Variable gross margin		$110.0
Sunk costs		
Manufacturing costs	$30.0	
Selling and administrative expenses	20.0	
Marketing media/promotion expense	22.0	72.0
Net income		$ 38.0

Studies in the past have repeatedly shown that marketing, including distribution, accounts for over 60¢ of every sales dollar. Exhibit 2 easily ignores the importance of the marketing and distribution function by emphasizing marginal analysis of manufacturing costs and, at the same time, lumping selling and administrative expenses as well as marketing, media, and promotional expenses.

THE BENEFITS OF RELEVANT COSTING

In order to trace the evolution of absorption costing and direct costing into the next step of sophistication, relevant costing, a composite Exhibit 3 is shown. Essentially it is the same as Exhibit 1, except that the composition of expenses within Exhibit 1 has been changed and placed elsewhere in the decision statement according to the logic of the decision level.

EXHIBIT 3   Augmented Contribution Margin Profit and Loss Statement

Proceeds from sales				$250.0
		Raw materials	40.0	
Variable cost of goods sold	120.0	Packing materials	20.0	
		Direct labor	60.0	
Variable gross profit (manufacturing contribution margin)				130.0
		Freight	5.0	
		Warehousing	6.0	
Other variable expense	20.0	Spoilage	2.0	
		Commissions	4.0	
		Discounts	3.0	
Variable profit (distribution contribution margin)				110.0
Direct product costs	22.0	Advertising	12.0	
		Promotion	10.0	
Direct product profit				88.0
		Sales management	0.7	
		Product management	0.3	
Direct division costs	4.5	Sales force	2.8	
		Sales incentive plan	0.2	
		Market research	0.5	
Division profit contribution (net contribution margin)				83.5
Allocated period expense		Supervisory	20.0	
Factory overhead	28.0	Maintenance	5.0	
Plant depreciation	5.0	Utilities, etc.	3.0	
		Administration	10.0	
		Bad debts	0.5	
Corporate administration, other	12.5	Interest	1.0	
		Branch office	1.0	
Net division profit (before taxes)				$ 38.0

Under relevant costing, charges are segregated into two categories:

1. Direct costs or product costs incurred because goods have been produced.

2. Indirect costs or period costs incurred on account of being in business but which are independent of the volume of the product.

Direct costs are those additional costs which are attributable to the existence of a product. This type of cost has a variable component, namely direct labor, direct material, and any other variable expense which is dependent on volume levels. The remainder of costs are attributable to a product or product lines existence, but *do not necessarily vary* with volume. The resultant of the first component, variability, is "variable profit." The resultant of the cumulative effect of all direct costs is "direct profit."

In the composite statement, gross profit has been replaced by a concept called "manufacturing contribution margin" which gives effect to the variable nature of raw materials, packing materials, and direct labor. The result, expressed on a unit basis, should easily answer the question presented earlier about the effect on profits of a change in volume. For example, if the manufacturing contribution margin per unit is 30¢, then the effect of increasing the sales of a product from 10,000 to 11,000 units would be $300. It also provides the vehicle for instantaneous break-even analysis. One need no longer require the presentation of graphics (the usual chart with a horizontal line representing fixed costs, a line at 45 degrees representing sales, and an additional line representing total costs) in order to arrive at break-even unit numbers. In the above instance with a 30¢ per unit variable profit rate, it would take the production of 1000 additional units to offset an incremental increase of $300 in period costs.

Notice that in Exhibit 3, allocated period expenses relating to the factory, mainly factory overhead and plant depreciation, have been taken out of their conventional place in the category "cost of goods sold" and placed far down below the division profit contribution level. The level *variable profit* is then truly an incremental amount of profit which accrues to each unit of sales. Below that level of profit, direct product costs have been isolated. Note that advertising and promotion are both classified as direct product cost in Exhibit 3. The prior discussion notwithstanding, there can be reasons why promotions, especially, are considered to be direct product costs but not variable with the number of units sold. The philosophy behind this rationale says that both media and promotions are established in terms of an annual dollar budget, and that there is a time limitation and a dollar top limitation for each of the expense categories. Therefore, they can never truly be variable with sales, except in very short time periods. The level of profit following direct product costs, called *direct profit,* in this context, *infers that this is the profit directly attributable to the existence of a product.*

Remember now that this is a composite decision statement, incorporating the results not only for a product but also for a division and the total company. Direct profit, as mentioned, is the profit for a product. What is needed now is a segregation of the incremental costs which are attributable to the existence of a division. This is classified in the category of direct division costs and includes sales management, product management, sales force, and the sales incentive plan. The logic of grouping these expenses under this category is synonymous with asking, "If I didn't have Product A, would I still have these division costs?" If the answer to the question is *yes,* then those expenses *are* attributable to the existence of the division but not to the existence of a particular product.

THE DIFFERING BEHAVIOR OF COSTS

The profit level called division profit contribution is that profit attributable to the existence of that division. The expenses below the divisional contribution level are basically all other period costs which have not been assigned to divisions. By inference, they owe their existence to the corporate structure and, in a sense, are a penalty for being in business. In a concrete sense, the easiest way to visualize what we are attempting to achieve by way of output from the foregoing discussion is shown in Exhibit 4. The exhibit shows the transition of Product Alpha from a level of 10,000 units to a level of 15,000 units. It is easy in this type of simplified schedule to segregate those expenses

EXHIBIT 4   The Differing Behavior of Costs

	Per Pound	Dollars
Product Alpha—10,000 Units		
Direct material	0.05	$ 500
Direct labor	0.02	200
Advertising	0.10	1000
Promotion	0.20	2000
Factory overhead	0.01	100
Product Alpha—15,000 Units		
Direct material	0.05	$ 750
Direct labor	0.02	300
Advertising	0.068	1000
Promotion[a]	0.20	3000
Factory overhead	0.006	100

[a] For specified period of time only unless the promotion is constant.

which might vary directly with the volume of the product. Direct material, direct labor, and promotions, in this case, are assumed to vary directly with the product. Advertising and factory overhead are considered to be in the nature of period costs. Note that when Product Alpha increases its volume to 15,000 units, the per unit rate for direct materials, direct labor, and promotions remains constant but the *dollars of expense change*. By the same token, advertising and factory overhead, because of their period nature, change when expressed in terms of units while the *dollars remain constant* in our decision statements.

IMPROVED EVALUATION OF MARKETING ALTERNATIVES

Another type of benefit to be gained by the type of relevant costing statement shown earlier in Exhibit 3 is the relationship between changes in results stemming from alternative plans. In Exhibit 5, Plan A and Plan B each call for a different result based on different spending patterns for promotions. It can easily be seen that with an expenditure of $2000 in promotions, an

EXHIBIT 5   Evaluation of Alternatives Using Relevant Costing

	Plan A	Plan B	Increment
Pounds	10,000	12,000	2,000
Variable profit	$5,000	$6,000	$1,000
Promotions	$2,000	$2,500	$ 500

incremental variable profit of $5000 is generated under Plan A. Alternatively, for an expenditure of $2500, an incremental variable profit is generated under Plan B. Therefore, the benefit to be gained by going with Plan B is best seen in the relationship that for every dollar spent in marketing promotions, $2 of incremental profit will be generated. It should not be immediately inferred that Plan B is the better plan. Expressed in terms of return on investment, Plan A is superior to Plan B because promotions turn over 2.5 times whereas in Plan B they turn over at a rate of 2.4 times. In a sense, this is very much akin to a return on investment calculation.

In order to further illustrate the uses of the relevant costing technique and the meaning of the levels of profit called variable profit and direct profit, Exhibits 6 through 9, illustrate in a simplified form sample problems which are realistic and which are encountered in every business, every day of operation.

Relevant costing is a thoroughly modern approach to decision-making in the modern business environment. In order to derive maximum benefits from internal procedures, relevant costing should be an adjunct to direct costing. It must be emphasized that relevant costing by itself is not an accounting procedure but is an internal analysis format. It is most difficult to use relevant costing as a copartner with absorption costing. However, it is quite consonant with standard costing. There is literally no reason why any company cannot make use of the technique.

The maximum benefit to be derived from relevant costing will accrue to that company which has the characteristic of being decentralized with multiproducts and multiple divisions.

SAMPLE PROBLEMS AND SOLUTIONS USING RELEVANT COSTING

EXHIBIT 6

Problem 1[10]

Determine: Effect on profit before taxes (PBT) resulting from lower volume. Marketing and other expenses remain constant.

Given: Product C

Variable profit per unit — $2.166

Proposed volume reduction — 10,000 units

Solution: 10,000 units × $2.166 (Variable profit per unit) = $21,660 reduced profit before taxes (PBT)

Problem 2

Determine: Unit volume necessary to achieve desired PBT. Marketing and other expenses are variable.

Given: Product P
Desired PBT   — $350,000
Deals   — $0.50 per unit
Period expenses   — $374,000

Variable profit — $2.622

10 Problems 1 through 5 in Exhibits 6 through 8 in this work appeared in an article written by this author entitled "Improved Marketing Analysis of Profitability, Relevant Costs, and Life Cycles," in the June 1967 issue of *Financial Executive*.

Solution: Desired PBT   — $350,000
          Add: period expenses — 374,000
          Total to account for $724,000

          Variable profit per unit $2.622
          Less: deal per unit   0.50
          Adusted rate per unit $2.122

   $724,000 ÷ $2.122 = 341,000 units

EXHIBIT 7

Problem 3

Determine: Additional unit volume necessary to hold planned gross constant with a decrease in selling price.

Given: Product G
       Expected selling price decrease — $0.10 per unit

       Variable profit per unit — $2.309

       Current volume — 3,248,160 units
       Cash discount rate — 1.95% of gross selling price
       Gross profit — $6,268,000

Solution: 1. 3,248,160 units × $2.309 = $7,500,000

           2. Variable profit per unit $2.309
              Less: Price decrease $0.100
                    Cash discount   0.002   0.098
              Adjusted variable profit per unit $2.211

           3. $7,500,000 ÷ $2.211 = 3,392,130 units required to hold gross profit or additional volume of 143,970 units.

Problem 4

Determine: Additional volume required to hold PBT constant with an increase in marketing expenditures.

Given: Product R
       Marketing expense increase — $100,000

       Variable profit per unit — $2.533

Solution: $100,000 ÷ $2.533 = 39,000 additional units required to cover additional marketing expenditures.

EXHIBIT 8

Problem 5

Determine: Break-even volume with no change in costs.

Given: Product C

Variable profit per unit — $1.559

Current volume — 958,948
Variable profit (total dollars) — $1,495,000
PBT — ($295,000)

Solution: 1. $1,495,000 + $295,000 = $1,790,000
2. $1,790,000 ÷ $1.599 = 1,148,000 units to break even.

EXHIBIT 9 Illustration of Some Cost-Volume-Profit Computations Available Directly from a Relevant Costing Statement

Facts:		
Sales		$200,000
Direct variable costs		75,000
Variable profit		$125,000
Period costs		100,000
Profit		$ 25,000

Profit-volume ratio:

$$\frac{Sales - Direct\ variable\ costs}{Sales} = \frac{200,000 - 75,000}{200,000} = 62.5\%$$

Break-even volume of sales:

$$\frac{Period\ costs}{1 - Direct\ variable\ costs/sales} = \frac{100,000}{1 - 75,000/200,000\ Shilling} = \$160,000$$

Ratio of allocated (period) expenses to sales:

$$\frac{Period\ costs}{Sales} = \frac{100,000}{200,000} = 50\%$$

Margin of safety: Sales — Break-even volume = $200,000 — 160,000 = $40,000

CHAPTER | 3

Making the Operating Statement Useful at all Levels of Responsibility

No idea is worth explaining unless it can be shown to contain elements of usefulness. The quest for profitability pursued in the last chapter led us to the point where the concept was explored in terms of theory, rationale, and practical examples. The utility of the concept will become apparent as we explore varieties of operating statements and further probe the application of profitability to business transactions.

For purposes of expanding and exploding the profitability concept, we shall assume in the subsequent discussion that three levels of operating statements are required:

1. A *product* statement primarily used by the product manager.

2. A *division* statement for the division general manager who oversees groups of product managers.

3. A *corporate* statement for general staff officers.

PRODUCT OPERATING STATEMENTS

The first operating statement, the Product Budgeted Profit and Loss Account (Exhibit 10), is basically designed for management's use in assessing the contribution to the corporation of an individual product and the product manager responsible for the product.[11] Five columns are provided in the statement so that a progression of historical or planned results can be compared with some prior period or plan. Within each column, three types of aggregates are used. In one type of relationship, results are expressed on a per unit rate; in this particular statement, it is expressed in pounds. Other expressions are in terms of the actual dollar amounts or as a percent of sales. Note the vertical description of types of expenses. *Variable product expenses* are defined as those which will vary directly with the physical units of sales. Included in this category are the manufacturing costs for the product that was sold, freight, warehousing, spoilage, cash discount, distributor's discount, and commissions. The resultant of the subtraction of all of these expenses from sales proceeds produces a level of profit called a *variable profit*. This is the level which is incremental to a unit of sale. Thus, if the variable profit per unit were 50¢ a pound, the sale of one unit would bring into the company 50¢ at the level of profit before taxes. The sales of two units would produce $1.00; the sale of three units would produce $1.50 and so on.

Following that group of expenses is an additional grouping also attributable to the product but not directly variable with unit sales. These expenses are called direct product costs and include advertising, promotions, prior years' advertising and promotion charges or credits, and marketing research which is incremental to the product. The total of these expenses is called direct product costs and the resultant of subtracting this latter group from variable profit is called, *direct profit*. As indicated earlier, direct profit infers that this is the profit directly attributable to the existence of this product. Any decision to delete a particular product from the product line should also delete the amount of direct profit (or loss) shown at that level of the operating statement.

The category of promotions presents somewhat of a contradiction as handled in this type of statement. As indicated earlier, promotions can be variable with the number of units sold. The most simple example of this type of promotion is an off-invoice promotion where the direct account remits to the seller the list price, less the amount of the off-invoice allowance. In this particular case, promotions enjoy a double existence. They are

---

11 Exhibits 10 and 11 were originally contained in an article written by this author in the June 1967 issue of *Financial Executive* entitled, "Improved Marketing Analysis of Profitability, Relevant Costs, and Life Cycles."

variable with units of sale but only *over a short period of time*. Promotions are temporary inducements to the trade but they do not carry a permanent nature. If they should become permanent, then they are, in effect, reductions in list prices and not truly promotions. In order to recognize this dual existence, it is necessary to understand that promotional expenses have both a time limitation and a maximum budgetary limitation. In effect, there is the constraint of time and an upper dollar limit.

For an immediate short-term decision, therefore, it may be necessary to create yet another level of profit. This level of profit would be *variable profit, less promotions*. It is a level especially useful for computing break-even points for new product introductions in fractionated markets or in test market rollouts. From the overall annual point of view, however, considering that there *is* a promotion budget, the expense has been posited as a direct product cost and, expressing it in terms of its *annual* impact, nonvariable with the units of sale.

Concession is made in this example of the operating statement to those individuals who believe that all costs must be allocated and that products truly have a level of profit called *net profit*. There is a provision on the statement to allocate any costs which may deem to be desirable. The author strongly disagrees with this technique. However, there are those individuals who simply cannot understand the financial statement which does not recognize all costs. Nevertheless, the decision-making level of profit is the *direct profit*.

The net profit level for any individual product is a completely specious level for making decisions. If a level of profit can be changed merely by changing the basis for allocation and if one can produce two or three or four net profits for the same product utilizing the same basic inputs, then it is hardly a vehicle for creating marketing or financial strategy. At this point, the reader may be well advised to again view Exhibit 3 in Chapter 2 so that he can relate *this product* operating statement with the *total* concept of a contribution margin operating statement as shown in that exhibit.

THE PRODUCT MANAGER DILEMMA

The reader should be under no illusions about this operating statement. It skirts a great many problems. Recall that earlier it was said that the prime use of this statement is for purposes of evaluating the performance of an individual product and *the performance of a product manager*. From the very beginning of this book, reference was made to the marketing concept and the evolution of the concept of the product manager. Much has been written about this position and a number of judgements can be made based on these observations. It has now become increasingly common for marketing personnel to be held responsible for the results of their areas expressed in quantitative terms. I think, though, that any dispassionate observer could reasonably question the propriety of this procedure and philosophy because there is reasonable doubt as to whether the product managers do have the ability to control their profit fate. There is a fine line of distinction between being held responsible for profits and being the prime influence on profit. The word control almost implies the unilateral right of decision-making and the ability to plan strategies to counteract seasonal, cyclical, and competitive movements in the market. It is akin to a divine right of decision-making.

In contrast, it is probably a truism that product managers can *influence* profits and profitability. With few exceptions, the consensus of writings and observations about the subject seems to indicate that the implementation of the product manager concept leaves a great deal to be desired. The decision-making dynamics of corporate life are extremely complicated and over a period of time, as understanding of the complexities of the business environment increases, it is almost inevitable that the objectives and responsibilities of the product manager's job will be defined much more clearly. Despite this, the fact remains that, quite often, the profit onus hits the product manager. At issue is the question of the fairness of this philosophy. The following tabulation summarizes the situation as the author sees it:

Marketing policy can directly influence:	*Marketing policy does not directly influence:*
Volume	Raw material prices
Sales Dollars—Volume	Cash discounts
—Price	Commissions
—Size mix	Other period expenses
Manufacturing cost—Volume	
—Level production	
—Inventories	
—Geographic selling pattern	
Variable costs—Freight	
—Warehousing	
Advertising and promotion	
Period factory expense—Throughput	
Direct divisional expense	

For the most part, the product manager cannot purchase raw materials. This is usually a function of the purchasing agent. If he were to go into a major manufacturing plant and ask John Smith to turn up his machine so that output would be twice as much as it is currently, it is probable that not only would he have the union shop steward on his neck, but he would also have the general manager of manufacturing. In many cases, firms are hiring advertising managers and this, in essence, precludes the product manager from completely choosing his own media programs. Further, it is likely that if the product manager controls a major product, one of the large ones within a company sphere, it is extremely doubtful if he can unilaterally affect significant price changes. The much bigger truth and this is something that marketing, as a discipline, has been loathe to admit, is that any product truly has many product managers. It may be the product manager himself, the division manager, the manufacturing manager, the purchasing or production manager and, certainly, the head of the company.

If the academic trapping are taken off the personification of the product manager, he emerges as an individual who can exert a great influence on the volume of his product and the promotional activity for his product. Indirectly, he will also affect *working capital,* those funds needed to keep the product going in the market once it has been established.

RELATIONSHIP BETWEEN THE PRODUCT MANAGER AND THE OPERATING STATEMENT

Because the product manager concept is integrally related with the operating statement as shown and almost all of the subsequent discussions regarding profitability, it is essential that the reader have an understanding of the way the concept is practiced in the modern business environment. An adjunct of the earlier mentioned research (Chapter 1) was to inquire into the marketing and financial relationships which existed within the twenty large companies interviewed.

Much has been written about the product manager but few individuals have presented the overview as effectively as Clarence Eldridge has done in his essay series entitled *The Management of the Marketing Function.*[12] Many of the problems which arose from the concept of the product manager system as practiced came from the responsibility point of view and, as a

---

[12] Clarence E. Eldridge, *The Management of the Marketing Function, Sixteen Essays.* New York, Association of National Advertisers, 1966.

result, more and more young people were being assigned to this type of position. Eldridge disagreed and posited the product manager on a status akin to a marketing director implying that the man is really not a youthful trainee, but a mature marketing man with considerable experience. Eldridge felt that the man's primary responsibility should be in advertising and, because of the failure to maintain standards for the position, the marketing director has not been able to delegate tasks. Eldridge concluded that as a result of this, the product manager system has failed its purpose.

Of the twenty companies interviewed in the research effort, fifteen of them replied that they do employ the product manager system. The results are shown in Table IV. The participants in the study were asked whether

TABLE IV   Companies Employing a Product Manager System

System	Number of Companies	Percentage of Total
Product manager	15	75
Other systems	5	25
	20	100

their product managers were held responsible for profits. Their replies are shown in Table V.

TABLE V   Profit Responsibility Under Product Manager System

Responsibility	Number of Companies	Percentage of Total
Responsibility for profit	10	65
Not responsible for profit	5	35
	15	100

Among the ten companies claiming to operate under a product manager system whereby the product manager is responsible for profit, most took a realistic view of the limitations of that responsibility for profit. The reply from Company A, a tobacco and food company, called attention to the fact that they may also be responsible for "non-profit." They conceded that ultimately the product manager is responsible for profits but that, in the short run, responsibility must be tempered, since quite often the man may be riding herd on a new product which involves heavy investment spending, precluding profitable operation. Their perspective view is that it is more proper to state that the man is responsible for adherence to the profit plan.

Company L rationalize.1 that the product manager is held responsible for profits only in a staff capacity. They felt that division managers have the real responsibility because the "job of moving the merchandise" truly lies with the head of the division.

Company P, a paper products company, conceded the weakness of its position. They stated that product managers are often held responsible for profits because "the things that they do affect profits." In a bit of self-rationalizing, though, they added that "in terms of the decision-making ability to affect profit, the answer must ultimately be no." The company did not care to comment further about the ambivalence of their statement and the fact that their product men are being judged on the basis of something they cannot control.

Company T, a pharmaceutical company, stated that even though the product manager was being held to account for product profits, it was really a team effort and the responsibility of the entire division. They conceded that the man has limited influence in manufacturing and he is not responsible for the sales force. He can initiate packaging changes and influence advertising and promotion policy. In a gross understatement, they added that "even if it isn't the fairest system, it's the most efficient." In an effort to confuse their position, they spoke further of their philosophy of responsibility and added that the man's performance does not rise or fall completely on profit attainment but is also influenced by the quality of his efforts in other areas of the marketing mix. Towards the close, they confessed that he was *not* "literally responsible for profits." According to them, he is responsible within the framework of the world in which he lives.

Company M, a food and confectionery company, was equally frank but less confused and spoke about the relative impotence of the product manager. They recognize that the man cannot control the elements of profit and that it is probably a fiction to ascribe that attribute to the man. They felt it was reasonable to simply say that they affect profits through their actions.

Company B, in their reply, took pains to point out that their product men are responsible for maintaining the profit plan and that, in the strict sense, they are not held accountable for profit variations. They pointed out that their product men's responsibilities are set forth in writing. These are the following:

Marketing Function	*Responsibility*
Development	Responsible for collecting, evaluating, and *circulating* all product information generated by the department and by services outside the

department for inclusion in the Brand Book. This includes Field Sales, Advertising, Market Research, Management Assignments, Competitive Information, etc.

Sales forecasts

Evaluates and recommends product goals and develops sales forecasts according to established procedures.

Development of objectives

Develops and proposes broad brand objectives and, consulting with appropriate departments, specific objectives for Sales, Promotion, Price, Publicity, and Packaging.

Determine advertising and sales promotion budgets

Serves and assists.

Advertising strategy

The development of the broad advertising approach including the creative and media strategy will be the function of a Strategy Committee, consisting of the Vice President —Marketing, the Marketing Manager, the Product Manager, and the Agency.

Media strategy framework

Collaborates.

Scheduling of media by area and timing within strategy framework

Initiates and collaborates.

Promotion planning

Develops and proposes.

Company D, a canner and processor, was one of the companies who claimed to have a product manager system but whose product men were not responsible for profit. Their reply makes plain the reason why:

Profit objectives are established in the Controller's area. Prices are established in the Controller's area also, on the basis of a stipulated profit goal on a full cost basis. The goal is approximately 7% net after taxes.

The conclusion is inescapable that this question posed a great deal of difficulty for the respondents because it forced most of them to support an unsupportable position. Two points are worthy of immediate exploration by the companies.

1. Those who wish to continue to hold the product manager responsible

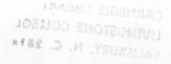

for profits of his product should consider charging against the product a standard cost which would not vary because of price or manufacturing efficiency variances. Another area of exploration could be an innovative operating statement utilizing only the operating costs for direct controllable marketing expenses, interest cost on inventories (if incremental), and interest cost on accounts receivable. If the product man controls distribution and elements of warehousing, a variant of these should be included.

2. Specifically delineated responsibilities such as those put forth by Company B could relieve some of the uncertainties in measuring job performance.

HOW THE PRODUCT MANAGER'S PERFORMANCE CAN BE MEASURED

The foregoing discussion concerning the results of the research study and the contemporary view of the responsibilities of the product manager has demonstrated that new processes of logic and financial techniques are needed to assess this unique type of "caretaker" position.

The operating statement for a product, Exhibit 10, contains elements within its presentation which enables a direct correlation between the financial performance of a product and the responsibility exercised by the product manager. The *direct profit* level on the operating statement isolates the incremental profit which exists because of the performance of the product. The product in turn is responsible to the actions of the product manager. In addition to that level of profit, the variable profit level on the statement shows the effect of strategies adopted by the product manager. It accomplishes this by measuring the incremental, financial results stemming from changes in volume, prices, costs, and mix influence. Further, the statement provides the base upon which a type of return on investment calculation can be applied against the jurisdiction of the product manager. That calculation, which is discussed in Chapter 9, requires two complementary measures to be related to each other—a return (represented by direct profit) and an investment (represented by the elements of working capital which can be *influenced* by the product manager).

DIVISION OPERATING STATEMENTS

Exhibit 11 is a Division Budgeted Profit and Loss Statement. It is constructed so that it follows smoothly from Exhibit 10. Note that about halfway

EXHIBIT 10 Product Budgeted Profit and Loss Statement

PRODUCT BUDGETED

	Revision II 19 / 19			Revision I 19 / 19		
	PER LB.	AMOUNT	%	PER LB.	AMOUNT	%
Budget Sales Units - Pounds						
Bonus Goods - Pounds						
TOTAL						
Net Proceeds from Sales						
Variable Cost of Goods Sold						
Freight and Charges						
Warehouse Expenses						
Spoiled Goods						
Cash Discount						
Distributors' Discount						
Commissions						
VARIABLE PROFIT						
Advertising - Media						
Promotions						
Promotions						
SUB-TOTAL						
Extraordinary Promotions						
Prior Years Adv./Promotion . .						
Market Research						
Other						
TOTAL DIRECT PRODUCT COST .						
DIRECT PROFIT						
Less Provision for Contingency						
NET DIRECT PROFIT						
Period Factory Expenses						
Direct Divisional Expenses						
Other Period Expenses						
NET PROFIT (LOSS)						

(Left margin labels: VARIABLE PRODUCT EXPENSES; DIRECT PRODUCT COST)

RAW MATERIAL ASSUMPTIONS:

$ _____ $ _____

Comments. _____

Financial Analysis and Planning - By_____ Date_____

PROFIT AND LOSS ACCOUNT

Product _____

| Original 19 | | | | | | | | |
| 19 | | | | | | | | |

PER LB.	AMOUNT	%	PER LB.	AMOUNT	%	PER LB.	AMOUNT	%

$ _____

$ _____

$ _____

Product _____ Rev. _____ Page No. _____

55

down on the vertical column of the statement is a recapitulation of *net direct profit*. There is merely a consolidation of all of the individual product operating statements up until that point. The basic difference about this statement is that direct divisional expenses are added so that a level called *division profit contribution* can be created. This level of profit is the profit which exists because the division exists. In other words, if the division were to be dissolved, all of the profit (or loss) which shows on that line would be eliminated. Since the division expenses are to be considered as *incremental* to the division, they would include such items as the expense of the divisional sales force, the sales incentive plan costs, and sales management period costs for the division. In addition, marketing general management expense in the person of the general manager of the division and his immediate staff are also represented. Some divisions have their own expenses for new product development which are separate and apart from corporate staff activity. The example shown in Exhibit 11 assumes that the division has its own incremental new product expense. As in the previous example (Exhibit 10), provision is made for the allocation of corporate period expenses if this is deemed to be desirable. Again, as in the previous instance, it must be emphasized that the decision-making level for divisional problems is the division profit contribution and decidedly *not* the net division profit, the amount which is the residual after allocations.

CORPORATE OPERATING STATEMENT

The last statement, Exhibit 12, is an example of an operating statement for the entire corporation. Note the progression on the statement from the product operating statement through the division operating statement down to the total corporate picture. In the vertical column, the level called *net direct profit* is the consolidation of that same level based upon the division operating statements, which in turn were based upon the sum total of the individual products. The level called division profit contribution is likewise a consolidation of that level from all of the division statements. At this point in the corporate operating statement, the allocation of period expenses disappears as a problem to be solved.

Following the level of profit represented by the division profit contribution, certain corporate expenses are highlighted. They include period factory expenses, plant depreciation, delineated on both a straight-line and an accelerated basis, general expenses, branch office expenses, representing sales offices and other types of distribution centers, specific sales office expenses not included in branch office expense, and interest on borrowed funds. In addition to these amounts, the variances from the standard performance for factory operations are shown as well as the corporate *staff* new products technical efforts. The reader is again advised to return to Exhibit 3, Chapter 2, so that he may compare the condensed aggregate operating statement with the individual configurations of each of the three which have just been presented.

REINFORCING THE PROFITABILITY CONCEPT

All of the foregoing illustrative materials contain within their construction, elements of the profitability concept as it applies to products, divisions, and to the total company concept. It is a simple enough matter to work backward from the vertical titles shown on the statements to the construction of a useful company-wide chart of accounting definitions which would accommodate the statistics of these statements. It is another matter, however, to take these statements and visualize going forward into decision situations and applying the principles of profitability. At this point, it is well to consider that the principles of profitability, as expressed in this book, require nothing more than a refinement of logic and a disregard of many previously held accounting concepts, such as the magic value of "gross profit."

The following section is designed to acquaint the reader with some elements of statistical probabilities as they can apply in specific profitability situations. An extensive case example is cited which, if entered into by the reader, will make certain that the material presented thus far will be shown to be practical and highly useful.

PROBABILITIES IN MARKETING

At this point, it may be well for the reader to engage in a simple exercise which serves to reinforce the concept of profitability in his mind. The exercise which follows purposefully includes elements of simple, statistical probabilities and the use of this technique, in this type of problem, may serve to acquaint the reader with a fine, valuable device by means of which he can determine the accuracy of quantitative answers given to his questions.

What is referred to here is a process of sharpening what may otherwise be considered to be impulsive estimates in a given situation. The sharpening process takes place through the use of applications of the normal curve concept in statistical decision theory. The normal curve is a pattern which depicts the probable dispersal of a number of bits of information, *provided*

EXHIBIT 11   Division Budgeted Profit and Loss Statement

DIVISION BUDGETED PROFIT AND

	REVISION II 19 19			REVISION I		
	AMOUNT		%	AMOUNT		
Net Proceeds from Sale	$			$		
Variable Cost of Goods Sold						
Variable PRODUCT Expenses						
VARIABLE PROFIT						
Advertising — Media						
Advertising — Government Allocation						
Promotions						
Promotions						
SUB-TOTAL						
Extraordinary Promotions						
Prior Year's Adv./Promotion						
Market Research						
Other						
TOTAL DIRECT PRODUCT COST						
DIRECT PROFIT						
Less — Provision for Contigency						
NET DIRECT PROFIT						
Customer Cost						
Sales Force						
Sales Incentive Plan						
Sales Management						
Marketing General Management						
New Product Expense						
Sundry Charges and Credits						
SUB-TOTAL						
DIVISION PROFIT CONTR.						
Factory Overhead						
Plant Depreciation — Regular						
Plant Depreciation — Accelerated						
General Expenses						
Branch Office Expenses						
Interest						
SUB-TOTAL						
NET DIVISION PROFIT						

Labels on the left margin:

- DIRECT → PRODUCT COST
- DIRECT → DIVISIONAL EXPENSES
- ALLOCATED → PERIOD EXPENSES

Comments: _____

_____

(a) Variable Product Expenses include Freight, Warehouse, Spoiled Goods, Cash Discount,
(b) General Expenses include Administrative Expense, other Depreciation, and Bad Debts.

Financial Analysis and Planning — By _____ **Date** _____

LOSS ACCOUNT

DIVISION

19 19		ORIGINAL	19 19												
%		AMOUNT		%		AMOUNT		%		AMOUNT		%			
		$				$				$					

Distributors' Discounts and Commissions.

_____ Division _____ Page No. _____ Rev. _____

EXHIBIT 12   Consolidated Budgeted Profit and Loss Statement

	REVISION II 19 19			REVISION I		
	AMOUNT		%	AMOUNT		
Net Proceeds from Sales	$		100 .00	$		
Variable Cost of Goods Sold						
Variable PRODUCT Expenses						
VARIABLE PROFIT						
Advertising Media						
Promotions						
Promotions						
SUB-TOTAL						
Extraordinary Promotions						
Prior Years Adv./Promotion.................						
Market Research						
Other						
TOTAL DIRECT PRODUCT COST						
DIRECT PROFIT....................						
Less Provision for Contingency						
NET-DIRECT PROFIT..............						
Customer Cost:						
Sales Force Expenses						
Sales Management						
Marketing General Management						
New Product Expense						
Sundry Charges and Credits						
SUB-TOTAL						
DIVISION PROFIT CONTR.						
Miscellaneous Profit Contribution						
Profit Contribution						
TOTAL DIV. PROFIT CONTR.						
Factory Overhead						
Plant Depreciation - Regular						
Plant Depreciation - Accelerated						
General Expenses						
Branch Office Expenses						
Interest						
SUB-TOTAL						
NET DIVISION PROFIT						
Factory Variances						
Product Improvement						
Sundry Income and Expenses						
Other						
PRAT						
....						
Inventory Reserve Adjustments						
NET PROFIT BEFORE FED. INC. TAX						
Federal Income Taxes						
NET CORPORATE PROFIT........						

Left margin labels: DIRECT / PRODUCT GOST (DIRECT PRODUCT COST); DIRECT DIVISIONAL EXPENSES; ALLOCATED PERIOD EXPENSES; CORPORATE PERIOD EXPENSES

Financial Analysis and Planning — By _____ Date _____

CONSOLIDATED BUDGETED PROFIT AND LOSS ACCOUNT

19 19		ORIGINAL 19 19									
%		AMOUNT		%		AMOUNT		%		AMOUNT		%
100	00	$			100	00	$		100	00	$			100	00

_____ **Total Company Rev.** _____

they are randomly chosen. The configuration of a normal curve is approximately as shown in Fig. 2.

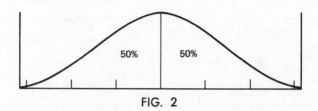

FIG. 2

Sometimes the curve is called a Bell curve or a Gaussian curve. If we transpose the configuration of the curve into numerical terms, it might be easier to understand the concept of simple intuitive probabilities. For example, if the sequence of numbers 2½, 5, 10, 20, 25, 20, 10, 5, and 2½ were plotted on a simple graph, they would appear as shown in Fig. 3. Note the resemblance of that pattern to the pattern of the normal curve.

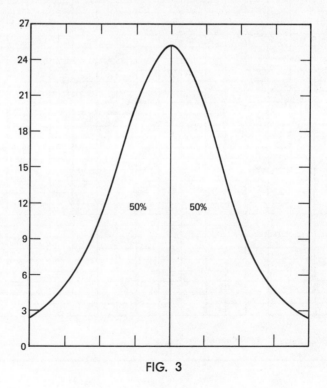

FIG. 3

It is a truism in statistics that certainty expressed in terms of the probability of occurrence can have a value no higher than 1 (or in effect 100%). If the pattern of numbers shown above to illustrate the normal curve pattern were expressed in terms of odds they might be written as follows:

$2\frac{1}{2}$ chances out of 100
5   chances out of 100
10   chances out of 100
20   chances out of 100
25   chances out of 100
20   chances out of 100
10   chances out of 100
5   chances out of 100
$2\frac{1}{2}$ chances out of 100

The total of the above odds equals 100% of certainty.

The next time you ask someone a question which brings a quick impulsive answer, test him with this little "sharpener." As an example, assume that the reader has asked one of his subordinates how many units of a given product he expects to sell and the subordinate quickly answers, 10,000 pounds. Set up a simple grid and ask the subordinate, *in terms of odds,* if there were only 5 chances in 100 of achieving his volume on the low side, what did he think he would sell. The subordinate might answer 8000 pounds. Ask again in terms of a better set of odds and question him by asking, if there were 25 chances in 100 on the low side, what would he sell. Assume the answer comes out to be 9000 pounds. This questioning could be continued until the number of chances in 100 totals 100 and also satisfies the rough pattern of a normal curve. The following example might show the comparison of such questioning as illustrated above:

Initial Volume Estimate—10,000 Pounds

5 chances in 100 it will be   8000
25 chances in 100 it will be   9000
35 chances in 100 it will be   9700
30 chances in 100 it will be   10,200
5 chances in 100 it will be   11,000

Note, that although the odds are not a perfect curve, they are reasonably approximate of the pattern. If each of the volumes is multiplied by the number of chances it has been assigned, it will, in effect, create a weighted average. On that basis, the answer to the problem is 9655 pounds.

CASE EXAMPLE OF THE
PROFITABILITY CONCEPT

A hypothetical situation has been created which poses a particular problem of alternatives before a given product manager in the Ultra Corporation. Simply stated, the problem is as follows:

Product manager, Joe Jones, associated with the packaged goods area, feels that there is untapped sales potential in Region 4. He has decided that with a little ingenuity he can create a "package deal" that will appeal to his customers thereby increasing sales and market penetration.

Accordingly, he establishes four alternative "packages" which contain one or more cases of different types of packs. These are detailed in part 1 and 2 of data supplied. Volume targets were established by him (part 3 of data) based upon his impression of the "salability" of the different alternatives. Promotional spending estimates for each "package" were determined by the composition of the package.

When the data were presented to the group product manager for evaluation, he asked Mr. Jones how reasonable his volume estimates were. In order to probe the volume estimates more deeply, he proposed that Mr. Jones evaluate varying volumes for each alternative based on simple intuitive probabilities. The results of Jones' evaluation are shown in part 4 of the given data.

1. From a quantitative approach, which alternative produces the largest direct profit?

2. Which alternative spends marketing money most efficiently?

3. Suppose the sales manager feels that there is more risk from a customer acceptance point of view for alternatives C and D as opposed to alternatives A and B. Should the probability be changed to reflect his opinion?

The specific quantitative input for the problem follows:

1. *Per Case*	24 Count Vanilla	24 Count Strawberry	26 Count Krispy	Assorted 1234	Assorted 3456
Selling price	$20.00	$20.00	$18.00	$16.00	$22.00
Variable cost of sales	9.00	11.00	7.00	5.00	14.00
Other variable expenses	1.25	1.25	1.00	0.75	1.00
Promotions (direct)	0.50	0.75	0.50	0.25	0.75
Allocated advertising	0.25	0.25	0.75	–	0.50
Period factory expense	0.10	0.10	0.20	0.05	0.10
Other corporate allocated expense	0.10	0.10	0.30	0.05	0.05

2. *Promotion Alternatives*

   A. 2 cs. 24 count vanilla
       1 cs. 24 count strawberry
       3 cs. 26 count krispy
       1 cs. assorted 1234

   B. 1 cs. 24 count vanilla
       2 cs. 24 count strawberry
       3 cs. 26 count krispy
       1 cs. assorted 3456

   C. 1 cs. 24 count vanilla
       4 cs. 26 count krispy
       1 cs. 24 count strawberry
       1 cs. assorted 3456

   D. 2 cs. assorted 1234
       3 cs. 25 count strawberry
       1 cs. 26 count krispy
       1 cs. 24 count vanilla

3. *Volume Targets*

Alternative A	10,000 units
Alternative B	10,800 units
Alternative C	10,500 units
Alternative D	11,000 units

4. *Probability Assumptions*

Alternative A:
    5 chances in 100 that volume will be 7,000 cs.
    25 chances in 100 that volume will be 8,000 cs.
    35 chances in 100 that volume will be 9,000 cs.
    30 chances in 100 that volume will be 11,000 cs.
    5 chances in 100 that volume will be 12,000 cs.

Alternative B:
    5 chances in 100 that volume will be 8,000 cs.
    25 chances in 100 that volume will be 9,000 cs.
    35 chances in 100 that volume will be 10,000 cs.
    30 chances in 100 that volume will be 11,000 cs.
    5 chances in 100 that volume will be 12,000 cs.

Alternative C:
    5 chances in 100 that volume will be 9,000 cs.
    25 chances in 100 that volume will be 9,500 cs.
    35 chances in 100 that volume will be 10,500 cs.
    30 chances in 100 that volume will be 11,000 cs.
    5 chances in 100 that volume will be 12,000 cs.

Alternative D:
    5 chances in 100 that volume will be 10,000 cs.
    25 chances in 100 that volume will be 10,500 cs.
    35 chances in 100 that volume will be 11,000 cs.
    30 chances in 100 that volume will be 12,000 cs.
    5 chances in 100 that volume will be 13,000 cs.

The solution to the problem is as follows:

Question 1, Step (a)

	Per Case				
	24 Count Vanilla	24 Count Strawberry	26 Count Krispy	Assorted 1234	Assorted 3456
Sales	$20.00	$20.00	$18.00	$16.00	$22.00
Cost of sales	9.00	11.00	7.00	5.00	14.00
Gross profit	$11.00	$ 9.00	$11.00	$11.00	$ 8.00
Variable expenses	1.25	1.25	1.00	0.75	1.00
Variable profit	$ 9.75	$ 7.75	$10.00	$10.25	$ 7.00
Promotion	0.50	0.75	0.50	0.25	0.75
Direct profit	$ 9.25	$ 7.00	$ 9.50	$10.00	$ 6.25

Question 1, Step (b)

Alternatives	Mix Comprised of (Per Above)					Total
A. Number of cases	2	1	3	1	—	
Direct profit	$18.50	$ 7.00	$28.50	$10.00	—	$64.00
B. Number of cases	1	2	3	—	1	
Direct profit	$ 9.25	$14.00	$28.50	—	$ 6.25	$58.00
C. Number of cases	1	1	4	—	1	
Direct profit	$ 9.25	$ 7.00	$38.00	—	$ 6.25	$60.50
D. Number of cases	1	3	1	2	—	
Direct profit	$ 9.25	$21.00	$ 9.50	$20.00	—	$59.75

Question 2

Promotion Spending Efficiency							
Mix Comprised of							

Alternatives	24 Count Vanilla	24 Count Strawberry	26 Count Krispy	Assorted 1234	Assorted 3456	Total	Efficiency Ratio
A. Number of cases	2	1	3	1	–	7	
Variable profit	$19.50	$ 7.75	$30.00	$10.25	–	$67.50	
Direct promotion	1.00	0.75	1.50	0.25	–	3.50	19.3 times
B. Number of cases	1	2	3	–	1	7	
Variable profit	$ 9.75	$15.50	$30.00	–	$ 7.00	$62.25	
Direct promotion	0.50	1.50	1.50	–	0.75	4.25	14.6 times
C. Number of cases	1	1	4	–	1	7	
Variable profit	$ 9.75	$ 7.75	$40.00	–	$ 7.00	$64.50	
Direct promotion	0.50	0.75	2.00	–	0.75	4.00	16.2 times
D. Number of cases	1	3	1	2	–	7	
Variable profit	$ 9.75	$23.25	$10.00	$20.50	–	$63.50	
Direct promotion	0.50	2.25	0.50	.50	–	3.75	16.9 times

Question 3

Alternative	Direct Profit (Based on Weighted Probable Volumes)
A	9,400 × $64.00 = $601.6
B	10,050 × $58.00 = $582.9
C	10,400 × $60.50 = $629.2
D	11,225 × $59.75 = $670.7

Alternative	Direct Profit (Based on Unweighted Volumes)
A	10,000 × $64.00 = $640.0
B	10,800 × $58.00 = $626.4
C	10,500 × $60.50 = $635.3
D	11,000 × $59.75 = $657.3

The foregoing problem and its solution should have served to solidify the probability concept if the reader properly attacked the problem. Simply using and understanding the profitability concept is not sufficient by itself to produce optimum decisions. The concept has many applications, including that of product life cycles, sales incentive plans, and return on investment problems. Succeeding chapters will explore these and other topics with regard to the application of the profitability concept.

| 4

Product Life Cycles and the Sources of Profit

I In the preceding two chapters the subject of profitability has been explored in the light of its concept and its applicability for operating statements. At this point, it is desirable to extend the horizon of the concept to a use which has not been fully exploited in marketing or financial profitability planning. This chapter will develop the concept, the theme, and the uses of the applicability of product life cycles to profitability planning and the "quality of profit."

THE QUALITY OF PROFIT

It is probable that most profit planning is done in a vacuum in that the planning does not take into account the length of time that an earnings flow is derived from a product. As a result, planners have not attuned themselves to inferring either a quality factor contained in each dollar of profit, nor have they considered a risk factor. Introducing the elements of quality and risk into a dialogue dealing with the subject of profit or profitability is something that is basically alien to modern, financial analytical theory. We are, after all, children of a capitalistic society and in a capitalistic society an appreciation of the *quantity* of profit is taught. It would be wearisome to remind the reader of the twenty-four million stockholders in the United States who daily peruse the financial pages of their newspapers to see whether the prices of their respective securities have risen or fallen. The root cause of ups and downs in stock prices is, of course, the profit impact which manifests itself in a number called earnings per share. As investors, all of us have been taught to appreciate the virtues of an ever higher earnings per share figure for our hero companies. Even internal managements view the success of divisions or total corporations in terms of rising earnings, as an indicator of good times. We have, therefore, been brought up with the American heritage that appreciates the quantity of profits as a measure of success. If earnings are rising, this is necessarily good.

At this point, the author would like to become antiestablishment and submit to the reader that this concept of appreciation of the quantity of profit may be rank nonsense and that a business which finds itself in the midst of a rising earnings pattern may be in serious trouble. It appears that pitifully few are concerned with the *quality* of profit. How *long* will we receive this flow of profits? What is its weighting in the product mix? How much of a contribution from growth products? From mature products? From declining products? From developmental products? What is the nature of the risk entailed in each life cycle category? Shouldn't profit be weighted for the degree of risk inherent in its formation?

After all, no one can seriously expect any product to hold a permanent place in the market. Products that did not exist ten years ago now account for up to 80% of volume in certain selected industries. How often has the reader gone into supermarkets to shop and looked at the variety of new cereal packages which are on the shelf compared to those which he knew only a relatively short time ago. The consumer in his insatiable desire for something new and his disposition toward tiring of things rather quickly has, in effect, forced upon producing companies the obligation to continuously provide a new stream of product concepts.

One must realistically ask if there is room in the marketplace for all of the old, established products *plus* the proliferation of the new product concepts. The answer is an obvious no. In the food industry, for example, for every 78 new products which are developed, 59 are rejected before they go to new products evaluation committees. At that point, 18 of the 19 remaining ideas are considered by the committee. By the end of the cycle, out of 60 new ideas which may develop at any one time, only one or two come to fruition. Despite this mortality rate, business continues to pour millions of dollars into research and development for new product concepts.

PRODUCT LIFE CYCLES

There is a direct relationship between the concept of profitability and the concept of profit life cycles. In order for the reader to understand this relationship, I will first discuss the general concept of life cycles. In this way, the part of the discussion concerning the practical applications of segregating the sources of profit into life cycles will be more easily understood.

By now, most sophisticated and thoughtful marketing people are familiar with the ideas that lie behind the concept of a product life cycle. Many marketing theorists agree that there is such a thing as a life cycle. Yet virtually no one has done anything about it. Product life cycles are like flying saucers; everyone has seen them but as yet no one has touched them. Exhibit 13 shows one conception of a life cycle. There are many other versions of life cycle conceptions which differ mainly in the delineation of cycle stages and in the terminology used. Most theorists, however, agree on what takes place in each stage of the life cycle.

EXHIBIT 13   Basic Life Cycle of Products

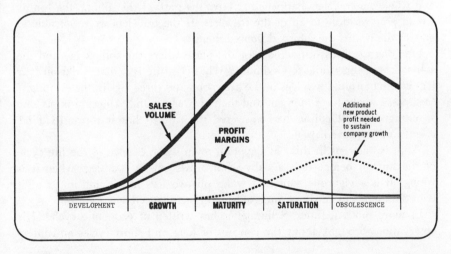

Recently, a study conducted by the A. C. Nielsen Company on a group of over 200 products of the Lever Brothers Corporation, found a numerical validity to the concept of life cycles. This study will be discussed more fully later in the chapter. In 1965, a study entitled "The American Soft Drink Industry and the Carbonated Beverage Market" was done by the Drs. Shih. One of their more interesting observations is reproduced in Exhibit 14.[13] This exhibit delved into the life cycle stages of various beverage industries and highlighted the growth stage of soft drinks relative to the "decadent" stage of coffee and tea.

The interesting implication here is that there are life cycles not only for products but also for such things as industries, flavors, and sizes. Of course, this is not a new revelation. Theodore Levitt has talked about the fact that marketing does not take sufficient advantage of the concept of product life cycles and plan in advance for stages of product cycles.

Thirty years ago, the then regular size of soft drinks (6 oz) commanded approximately 70% of the market share for the size mix—today, it is down to about 37%. Even coffee drinking, a great American pastime, is declining on a per capita basis. In fact, there is good evidence that the total coffee market is declining about 1% a year. Compact cars, after going out of style, are coming back into style again. Women's fashions, notably in the length of hemlines, are subject to cyclical popularity.

This discussion about life cycles has its roots in the antiquity of man. It should not really surprise anyone that life cycles have a profound influence not only on our marketing economy but also on our daily lives and decisions. An ancient Egyptian legend told about the wanderings of Oedipus in the desert. At that time, the sphinx was a living creature who roamed the desert and whenever travelers happened to cross the path of the sphinx, the sphinx would pose a riddle to all of the travelers. If the travelers were not able to answer the riddle, the sphinx devoured them.

One day Oedipus wandered past the place where the sphinx lay and the sphinx posed this riddle to Oedipus: "What creature is it that walks on four legs in the morning, two legs in the afternoon and three legs in the evening?" Oedipus thought for a moment and then answer, "man." The sphinx became so enraged that Oedipus had answered the riddle, that it threw itself off a cliff and destroyed itself.

What is inherent in this old Egyptian myth is the essence of the life cycle of the human being. It is a baby what crawls on its four legs when it is young; it is a vigorous man that walks on two legs in his mid-life, and it is an old man who needs a crutch to lean on in advanced age.

In more modern times, Schumpeter has written of economic cycles. His observations brought about the concept of long and short cycles and inter-

---

[13] Exhibit 14 "Life Cycles of Selected Beverages," was reproduced from a study entitled *American Soft Drink Industry and the Carbonated Beverage Market,* done by Drs. Ko Ching Shih and C. Ying Shih, 1965.

mediate cycles, all of which affect the economy at different times. Even now in the economic environment, we still tend to go through cycles of home building and family formations.

THE ORIGINS OF PRODUCT
LIFE CYCLE MODELS

The exact origins of the product life cycle model are unknown. The basic concept of an "S"-shaped growth curve probably originated with the world-known sociologist Gabriel Tarde around 1900. He found that a general pattern of this kind existed in the history of the adoption of various innovations. In 1920, the biologist Raymond Pearl published the results of his studies of population growth. Pearl found that the same basic "S" curve could be used to describe the growth and population of single-celled organisms and insects, as well as long-term trends in the human populations of the nations of the world. Raymond Pearl's work attracted considerable attention and, subsequently, the "S" curve came to be called the "law of growth" because it seemed to be applicable to so many kinds of growth.

The first application of the "S" curve model to the analysis of sales trends was probably made by the statistician Raymond Prescott in the early 1920s. He found that the model provided a good description of the historical trends in the sales of automobiles and other products. He even appeared to anticipate much of the later research on the diffusion of innovations in his suggestion that initial growth is slow because of the consumer's resistance to change and habits, while later growth may be rapid because of the influence exerted by "early adopters" on other consumers.

Since then, the product life cycle concept has become accepted as a regular part of marketing theory and many authors have gone to considerable lengths explaining the different stages of the product life cycle. So far, however, the concept has remained a theory with its place only in marketing textbooks and without having the distinction of practical value.

In a fine article a few years ago, Theodore Levitt[14] spoke of the origins and the subsequent cyclical stages of nylon as it was developed by the DuPont Company. He spoke originally of its development for wartime purposes, specifically for parachutes. He then traced the course of the life cycle of nylon through to women's stockings, embroidered women's stockings, automobile tires, fabrics, rugs, and so on. The lesson that Professor Levitt has attempted

---

14 Theodóre Levitt, "Exploit The Product Life Cycles," *Harvard Business Review*, Vol. 43, No. 6, Nov./Dec. 1965.

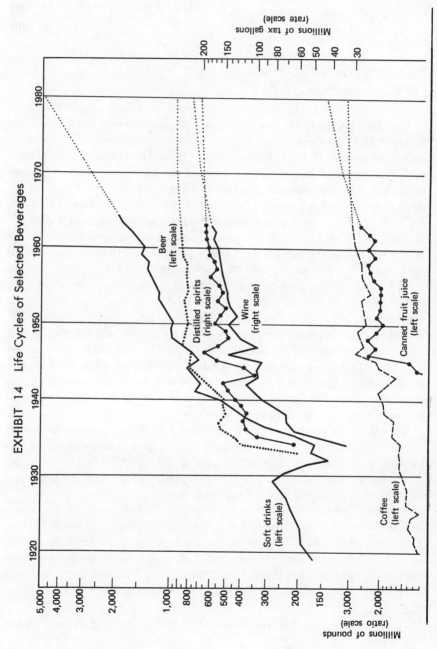

EXHIBIT 14 Life Cycles of Selected Beverages

Millions of tax gallons
(rate scale)

200
150
100
80
60
50
40
30

1980
1970
1960
1950
1940
1930
1920

Beer
(left scale)

Distilled spirits
(right scale)

Wine
(right scale)

Canned fruit juice
(left scale)

Soft drinks
(left scale)

Coffee
(left scale)

5,000
4,000
3,000
2,000

1,000
800
600
500
400

300

200
150

3,000

2,000

Millions of pounds
(ratio scale)

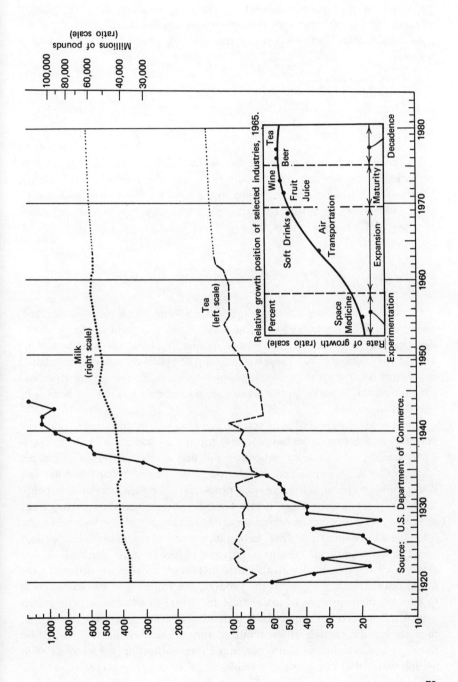

Millions of pounds (ratio scale)

Milk (right scale)

Tea (left scale)

Relative growth position of selected industries, 1965.

Tea
Wine   Beer
Fruit
Juice
Soft Drinks
Air
Transportation
Space
Medicine
Percent

Rate of growth (ratio scale)

Experimentation   Expansion   Maturity   Decadence

Source: U.S. Department of Commerce.

75

to preach is that proper marketing planning requires that we plan in advance for the various stages through which a product will live.

In common uses, these phases of the life of a product are thought of as follows:

1. Developmental
2. Growth
3. Maturity
4. Saturation
5. Decline

Within each of these stages of the life cycle of a product, a great deal of varied economic activity goes on. Although the author is certain that there will be differences of opinion as to the specifics of activities within each of the life cycle stages, the following discussion is a representative picture of activity within cycle phases.

DEVELOPMENTAL STAGE

In the *developmental* stage of a product, the objective is to introduce, test, and make the consumer aware of the product. At this point in the product's development, there is no demand for it other than by those who may be termed the high mobiles. These are a group of relatively affluent, influential individuals who are, in essence, influence creators. They are the style and pace setters for demand. In this stage also, the product has not yet been fully tested or approved.

Because awareness and acceptance are minimal in this stage, sales rise very slowly and pricing techniques tend toward a "skimming" policy. Excellent examples of this occurred when the first electric knives and electric toothbrushes were introduced at relatively high prices. Since there are few direct competitors at this stage of a product's life cycle, it is, at this point, that the greatest advantage accrues to the innovator who produces the product. The phenomenon which occurs at this stage is that consumers quite often have to be unlearned from habitual patterns. Many product innovations break down traditional consumer patterns of behavior or demand. A fine example of this occurred with the introduction of freeze-dried coffee. In the initial test-marketing stages for the product, the emphasis of media copy was to educate the consumer to understand the freeze-dried process. The reader may recall advertising copy which showed coffee being brewed frozen and then having the crystals of ice removed through a vacuum. Only then did the copy indicate to the consumer that by reconstituting the product with boiling water that the flavor of percolated coffee could be recreated.

Marketing costs in this stage of development also are uniquely high because of the introductory expenses involved, especially those dealing with promotional activities which encourage dealer loading for new products. Mainly because of this fact and manufacturing inefficiencies, which still exist, product profit margins tend to be quite low and, in fact, it is not uncommon at all for many new products to incur substantial losses during this stage of their life cycle.

A study in 1959 (Exhibit 15) by the Finnish economist Gösta Mickwitz provided an interesting insight on a conceptual basis of the prime influences on the elasticity of various marketing devices during various stages of a product's success. Following in order were media efforts, pricing policy and, lastly, service considerations.

EXHIBIT 15   Market Mix Impact by Life Cycle Stages

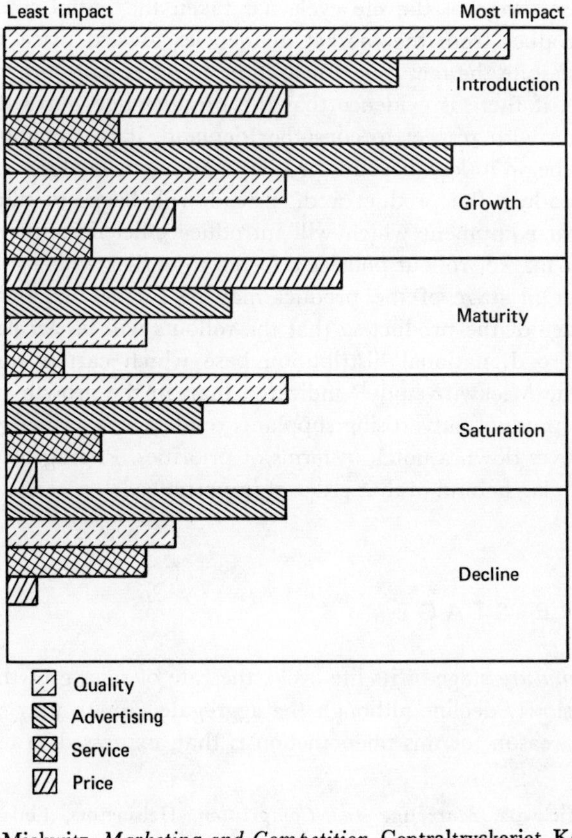

Based on Gösta Mickwitz, *Marketing and Competition,* Centraltryckeriet, Kelsing+fors, Finland, 1959.

GROWTH STAGE

The next phase of a product's life might be considered as the *growth* phase. Sales growth accelerates; this may be due to word-of-mouth influence, possibly from the high mobiles referred to earlier. Initially high introductory marketing expenses have been invested in the product and efforts are intensified to provide a broader distribution base. At this point, an initial acceptance for the product has been established in the market. It is not uncommon to see competitors attempting to copy the product and introduce their own versions with slightly unique features. Examples of this occurred with the electric toothbrush, when General Electric found itself in competition with Squibb, and with the electric knife, when Sunbeam and General Electric came into competition.

This tendency towards competition generally produces some ancillary effects. Once the skimming policy of pricing which was developed in the development stage of the life cycle has taken the initial consumer demand for the product from the market, tendencies toward price softening begin to occur, despite the fact that distribution becomes more broad-based. At the same time, if there is evidence that the product does have the potential of catching on with respect to consumer demand, it is probable that the producer will begin to look beyond the pilot equipment facilities which are being used to produce the product and, instead, will begin to think in terms of longer term equipment which will introduce efficiencies in manufacturing.

The test-market rollout policies referred to earlier which take place in the developmental stage of the product may be further expanded during the growth stage of the product so that the rollouts will be accelerated and will create a broad, national distribution base which carries sales momentum with it. The Mickwitz study[15] indicated that, in the growth stage of the life cycle of a product, advertising supplants quality as a primary influence and quality moves down a notch in terms of priorities. Pricing policy and service continue to lag behind in that order of importance.

MATURE STAGE

In the *mature* stage of its life cycle, the rate of sales growth for a product begins to slowly decline although the aggregate growth may still be present. The main reason for this phenomenon is that, expressed in terms of market

---

[15] Gösta Mickwitz, *Marketing and Competition.* Helsingfors, Finland, Centraltryckeriet, 1959.

segmentation, the audience at which the product was directed has largely been contacted and the essential demand has been satisfied. The prime customer base in this stage of the life cycle is new family formations. In essence, they create a cycle within a cycle in that the awareness on the part of the new family formation is similar to that of the original consumers in the latter part of the developmental and growth stages. The product characteristic of this stage of the life cycle is that products tend to become indistinguishable from one another. An excellent example of the mature stage of the life cycle is the homogeneity of gasolines. Studies of octane content of gasolines have shown that there is usually no more than a 1- or 2-point octane differential between major brands. Therefore, the marketing techniques used to attract the consumers to individual brands have necessarily depended upon those messages which will create a distinction in the mind of the consumer. This may be done through the route of additives, games of chance, or through abstract symbols such as Esso Gasoline who put a tiger in their tank.

Because mass distribution has been accomplished at this stage in the life cycle, quite often *de facto* price declines begin to take place with a consequent shrinkage in profit margins in order to encourage the growth of volume. The *de facto* price declines may take the form of alterations of trade selling terms, specific trade promotions, or the actual price decline itself in terms of listed prices. It is common at this stage of the life cycle also for selected specialty producers to come into being. Quite often when a product is homogenous with others and the requirement is for a distinction to be created, that distinction is generated by means of upgrading the product. A common example of this is found in the market for ball-point pens where specialty producers manufacture ball-point pen desk sets that are priced substantially higher than the average ball-point pen.

At this point also, many manufacturers tend to establish their own private branded labels. Many restaurant chains desire to sell their own coffee even though it is quite often made by one of the leading manufacturers of the mature branded coffee product. At some time in this life cycle stage, the phenomenon of annual models and trade-ins begins to appear and quite often this need for retooling and redesigning has the effect of shaking out competitors. This is the point in the cycle when the well capitalized manufacturer can still exist. Those which are under-capitalized will reach their critical stages during this phase of the life cycle.

It would be logical to assume, in view of the homogeneity of products in this stage of the life cycle, that price would displace advertising as the strongest influence on product success. This is confirmed by the Mickwitz report which indicates that in order of priority of importance, the influences affecting products during this stage are price, advertising, quality, and service.

SATURATION STAGE

The next to the last phase of the product life cycle has been termed as the *saturation* stage. Actually this is characterized by a more rapid shrinking of profit margins because there is a decreasing return on investment, expressed in marginal terms. Increased advertising and promotional funds are needed to keep products alive in the face of the saturation of competition and, at this stage, it is incumbent upon most processors and manufacturers to ask themselves what the alternatives are to the present marketing policy. "Am I better off putting my money into another product?" Competition by this time has already been stabilized and this, of course, poses some very high entry barriers for potential competition to enter into the market. This would be expected given that there are already too many of the same types of products in the market. Quality might replace price as the prime influence towards a product's success. The Mickwitz's report expresses in terms of importance: quality, advertising, service, and price.

DECLINING STAGE

The last stage of the life cycle of a product has frequently been termed as the *declining* stage of the cycle, although some theorists prefer to call it the *obsolescence* stage. A unique feature in the life of a product takes place during this stage in that there tends to be a return to the original demand for the product. In other words, by that time, a hard core of users has been cultivated. As sales continue to decline, the competitive nature of the business for the product begins to lose its challenge. Many of the firms which were heretofore in avid competition begin to drop out and, quite often, the remaining producers are able to dispense with any further advertisements to communicate with the consumer. An excellent example of this type of marketing policy in the obsolescence stage of the life cycle can be found in the manner in which products such as LaFrance and Satina are marketed to the consumer. These products have really been superseded by more modern convenient products. There is, however, a hard core of users who continue to purchase the product. The marketing policy of General Foods has been to minimize as much as possible any advertising and promotional investments in the product. Despite this marketing policy on the part of the company, the product continues to sell to a small but steady audience.

The Mickwitz report concluded that at this stage of the life cycle, advertising exerts the greatest influence on product movement, followed in order by service, quality, and price considerations.

PRODUCT   REGENERATION

At this point, it would be nominally easy to accept the fact that the cycle of the product has run its course. In the real world of marketing and manufacturing, this is not necessarily the case. Further steps are possible to rejuvenate a product and they are generally considered under the generic term of *regeneration*. One of the many ways of regenerating a product which has apparently run its cycle is to find a new use for the same product. One newspaper columnist noted that a fabricator of machine nuts and bolts found that a certain rustproof nut and bolt sold very well on a seasonal basis. The company discovered that the reason for the excellent sales on a seasonal basis were that the bolt and the nut were found to be rustproof and that car owners were attaching them to license plates for cars. The company's action upon learning that was to package a nut and bolt kit specifically for the purpose of attaching license plates.

Further in that vein, chocolate morsels or bits, as they sometimes may be called, have traditionally been sold by food processing companies as an item for the home baking market. The avowed purpose of the item is for housewives to include the bits when they bake tollhouse cookies. Over the last few years, the market for home baking has suffered an attrition, mainly because of the rise of convenience foods and the abundance of quality prebaked products. The strategy employed by the major food processors producing chocolate bits is now beginning to turn towards educating the public to consider chocolate bits as a snack item and to encourage the consumer to make these bits available in a bowl or in an apothecary jar, or to have them for children's nibbles. All of this is much is the same vein that Professor Levitt alluded to in his tracing of the course of the life cycle of nylon referred to earlier.

Another technique used to regenerate a product is simply to restyle it. This is quite common, of course, in the auto industry and, in fact, in many durable consumer goods products such as television, refrigerators, washers, and dryers. Another approach is to create a type of "camp" appeal for a product. It is not uncommon to go into major home furnishing outlets in these days and be able to find a potbellied stove or at least a simulated potbellied stove. Tiffany lamps which were once out of style have now returned to style as a result of the creation of a demand for fashion which recreates the atmosphere of former days.

NIELSEN STUDY OF LIFE CYCLES

The traditional method of defining life cycle behavior has always been expressed in terms of the physical volume of a product. A very interesting study was conducted by the A. C. Nielsen Company[16] beginning in 1961. It studied over 275 brands of consumer products over a five-year period. The interesting facet of the study, aside from its conclusions, is that its definition of life cycles is expressed in terms of market share maintenance. Thirty-seven product classes which were handled in grocery outlets were used in this study. All three major, general product categories are represented in this study, including health and beauty aids, food products, and household products. Exhibit 16 outlines the list of the various product categories which were studied.

Another interesting approach of the Nielsen study was that sales curves were derived on a nonseasonal basis. In other words, seasonal fluctuations were smoothed out through statistical means. The Nielsen concept of life cycles introduced four new terms to marketing theory of cycles: ᐧ

1. Primary cycle
2. Recycle
3. Prolonged cycle
4. Incomplete life cycle

As defined in the study, the primary cycle is the initial cycle in the history of a new brand. This includes the introduction and initial period of growth or buildup to a crest, however short or long and, in addition, it also includes the subsequent leveling out period. The primary cycle cuts off where the leveling out dips below 80% of the crest of repeat buying. In terms of behavioral pattern, the Nielsen definition of the primary growth cycle encompasses the traditional cycles of development, growth, maturity, saturation, and decline. As can be noted in the Nielsen version of the life cycle of a product (Exhibit 17), the tailing off of volume for a product is not nearly as precitous as is generally held in the traditional configuration of the life cycle.

In evaluating the behavioral patterns of primary cycles, all brands of products that were introduced from 1961 and forward were included, with two important exceptions:

1. Those brands entering the market very late in 1965 or later which did not accumulate sufficient data for evaluation.

---

[16] *The Nielsen Researcher.* Chicago, Illinois, A. C. Nielsen Company, No. 1, 1968.

EXHIBIT 16   Product Categories Contained in Nielsen Study

Cosmetic and Health Aids
   Dentifrices
   After shave lotion
   Cough syrups
   Denture cleaners
   Deodorants
   Mouthwash
   Shaving cream
   Headache remedies

Household Products
   Scouring powders
   Dishwashing soaps
   Fabric softeners
   Detergents
   Bleaches
   Paper towels
   Toilet tissue
   Soap
   Floor wax
   Food wraps

Foods
   Pancake syrups
   Margarine
   Dry soup mixes
   Soft drinks
   Whipped toppings
   Cookies
   Peanut butter
   Ketchup
   Dog foods
   Cereals
   Shortenings
   Powdered soft drinks

2. Brands that were considered to be "immediate failures." The cutoff point for defining a failure is any brand that failed to hold 50% of its initial peak market share by the end of the first year of the market.

The second important term introduced to the life cycle concept by the Nielsen study is "recycle." The study defines this term as an significant nonseasonal improvement in share trend after the primary cycle which manifests itself either in:

1. An acceleration in an upward trend
2. A reversal of a previously declining trend
3. A slowing up of a declining trend.

EXHIBIT 17   Grocery Product Life Cycles

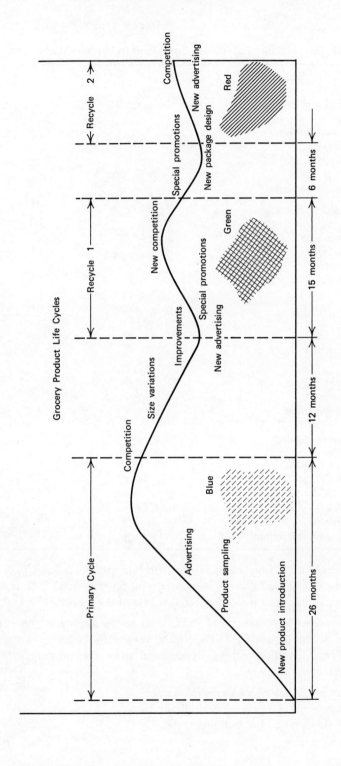

Grocery Product Life Cycles

Based on *The Nielsen Researcher*, A. C. Nielsen Company, Chicago, Ill. No. 1, 1968.

Each of these three options must have occurred as a result of either a planned effort or the unexpected benefit of a change in the competitive climate.

The study considered "prolonged cycles" as being composed of either of two types, "up cycle" which is indicative of a long-term improving trend, and "down cycle" which is a long-term down trend. Each of these is applicable to brands existing before 1961 which had protracted long-term trends in the same direction over most or all of the period in the study. These trends occurred where the so-called recycling efforts were not clearly discernible either in the acceleration of the strong trend of the slowing or reversal of the trend.

The objective of the entire study was to permit measurement of the various characteristics of the life cycle, including the duration, frequency, or variations in life cycle patterns which may occur because of the types of products being studied. In addition, factors were researched which might have an influence on the starting and the ending of a life cycle. As was mentioned earlier, the basic concept behind defining the life cycle of a product in the Nielsen study is expressed in terms of market share. The basic source data for the study was the bimonthly share trends of the 275 products included in this study. In addition, the Nielsen Food Index for the 35 product categories was used. Exhibit 18 shows a summary classification of the various brands reviewed, as well as the product category and type of life cycle for the brands.

The conclusions of the Nielsen study are somewhat startling in their impact on marketing planning. Two major observations are relevant toward the findings concerned with primary cycles:

1. The primary cycle for all of the new brands introduced between 1961 and the beginning of 1966 averaged slightly above 2 years. Only 15% of the brands continued to grow beyond 3 years.

2. Variations by product type existed. Food products tended to run slightly shorter cycles, whereas health and beauty aids tended to run slightly longer cycles. Household products centered around the average of all products. Exhibit 18 shows the average length and the spread of primary cycles for all product types.

The primary cycle for health and beauty aids extended between 10 months and 60 months with the average at 29 months. Food products had a range of cycle between 10 and 48 months with an average of 23 months. One of the most important conclusions reached by the study was the observation that the life expectancy of new brand introductions halved between 1961 and 1964. In 1961, the life expectancy of a new brand was approximately 3 years, whereas by 1964, that life expectancy had receded to 18 months.

In evaluating the importance of primary cycles, a critical analysis of the factors which influenced the closing of cycles is mandatory. The study being reviewed indicated that, by far, the most important factor bringing the

EXHIBIT 18   Life Cycle Stages of Grocery Products (1961-1965)[a]

	Foods	Household Products	Cosmetic and Health Aids	Aggregate
Primary cycles	20%	30%	29%	26%
Failures	7	—	1	3
Recycles	39	43	23	36
Up cycles (prolonged)	3	—	5	3
Down cycles (prolonged)	20	16	20	19
Other	11	11	22	13
Total	100%	100%	100%	100%

[a] Based upon the Neilsen study.

primary cycle of a brand to a close was the introduction of a new brand by competition. The second most important were events which were brought about by the action of the manufacturer itself. This may have taken the form of reductions in spending support or other various types of problems which may have arisen with the product.

Recycling efforts, as would be logically expected, were of a much shorter duration than the marketing effort which brought about the primary cycle. On an average, the initial recycling efforts were successful only for a period of one year. Moreover, the study found that each product had, on an average, 1.3 recycling efforts implying that, at best, the average length of total recycling efforts for any product was about 16 months. Although there were some differences noticed in recycling efforts by product type, the differences were insignificant in terms of an average for all products.

Given the short duration for the life of an average product, the implications of the quality of profit become even more important. Based upon the findings of the earlier studies of product life cycles and the later Nielsen report, it is evident that there must be a continuous stream of new product development in any corporation in order to ensure the stability and the sources of profit. It should be even more apparent now, after this discussion, that the economic concept of the monetary value of a dollar may not necessarily be completely indicative of the worth of the exchange medium. A dollar may not be a dollar. The profit that is derived from products in their developmental and growth stages may be worth far more to a corporation in terms of the longevity of the sources of that profit than is the profit which is derived from a mature or declining product.

It may be well at this point for the reader to look at a perspective of the implications of the observations just cited. The primary cycle averaged slightly longer than 2 years for the composite of 275 products within various product types. The initial *recycling* effort tended to run slightly longer than a year. Therefore, within the short span of 3 years, a product will have run *its stage of development, growth, maturity, saturation, and decline* and, in addition, will have required that additional marketing investment spending be used in support of the product. These observations should give pause to any executive concerned with the efficient use of research and development funds.

A further observation made by the study was that the average number of recycles per brand averaged about 1.3 times, further giving credence to the observation that the expected life of a new brand on an average will be about 3 years.

Recycling efforts in themselves are a technique set separate and apart from the basic primary cycle strategy. Sixty percent of the recycling effort was accomplished through the medium of advertising, either in the form of additional funds invested, or in copy changes, or in combinations of both. In the remaining 40% of the recycles, the advertising effort was keyed to a product improvement or innovation. However, the observation still remains that whatever the method or the vehicle for the recycling effort, the duration of improvement was about the same.

The odds for holding the share of an established brand over a five-year span through a continuous pattern of recycling efforts against the inroads of new brand competition, were found to be only 50–50, if expressed in terms of the market share. As an alternative, if we were to assume that the various brands which are in phases of prolonged cycles as a rough yardstick of minimum recycling efforts, the odds of holding the share of that brand's market reduced to about one chance in eight.

The implications of the above cited study on marketing strategy are quite consonant with the suggestions made by Theodore Levitt in his original article in 1965. The Nielsen study's conclusions revolve around two essential points:

1. There is a strong need for incorporating in brand strategy a "ready" plan for the first recycling effort which will almost certainly be required after the initial two years of the product's life. This planning effort should include alternatives sufficienty flexible to enable the product to meet and survive in a changing competitive climate.

2. The apparently short span of recycling efforts imposes an even greater obligation on the planner to establish a follow-up system whereby the planning discipline is created which will establish a "due" date for the next plan or change in marketing mix at least one year in advance.

PRACTICAL APPLICATIONS OF LIFE CYCLE THEORY

With the increasingly available insights gained by accelerated curiosity into the phenomenon of brand life cycles, *the extension of the theory of the concept into practical use* becomes even more important. An attempt was made in 1967 by the author to bring forth a quantitative technique to take advantage of life cycle theory. An article appeared in the *Financial Executive* magazine entitled "Improved Marketing Analysis of Profitability, Relevant Costs and Life Cycles." Included in the text was a sample of a worksheet which, if properly executed, would permit an analysis of profit by its source components. All of the discussion following will be an elaboration on the technique which was originally set forth in that article.

The initial challenge in quantitatively using life cycle theory is to create a method whereby the sources of profit can be segregated into life cycle stages.

Using an extremely simple illustration, we might take a commonly branded instant coffee. Expressed in aggregate terms, the profit importance of instant coffee can be substantial on large corporations. As an example, one of the largest food processors in the United States derives approximately 40% of its profit from its total coffee business which includes a substantial amount of instant coffee sales. The importance of the segregation of profits into life cycle stages lies in the area of proper allocation of marketing resources. The author earlier had maintained that profit planning tends to be conducted in a vacuum. In addition to the vacuumlike atmosphere, marketing planning is often constructed based on the bias of volume considerations and personal loyalties of brand managers toward their products. This is relatively understandable if a brand manager were to be unwilling to concede that his product is mature or declining, inferring that it may have a limited life with respect to profitaibility. It is very much like asking a product manager to condone disloyalty. The value of using life cycle theory to plan profits is that it permits marketing to direct its optimum placement of resources. Naturally, these are all longer term considerations and are really only in the context of a true profit plan, preferably spanning a time interval of three to five years.

Despite the importance of these types of profits to the company, an extremely pertinent question is, "how long might this stream of profits continue to be forthcoming for the company?" In terms of consumption habits, the market for total coffee is declining at approximately 1% per year and at the same time the consumption per capita, expressed in cups per day of coffee, is declining among the population. That same company, by the way, markets a very successful growth product which is a dessert topping. Volume has shown steady, dramatic improvement and it is an extremely profitable product. At this point, the author would ask the reader to consider whether the dollar of profit derived from the sale of coffee has the same value to the company *at this point* as the dollar of profit derived from the sale of the dessert product.

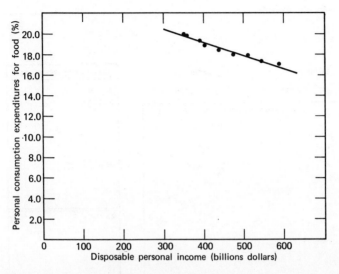

Source: National Food Situation, U.S. Department of Agriculture, February 1969, Table 2, p. 8.

Year	Disposable Personal Income (billions)	Consumer Spending for Food (%)
1960	$350.0	20.0
1961	364.4	19.8
1962	385.3	19.3
1963	404.6	18.9
1964	438.1	18.4
1965	473.2	18.1
1966	511.6	18.1
1967	546.3	17.4
1968	588.8	17.2

USING AGGREGATE STATISTICS

One of the ways of segregating profits into the life cycle stages from which it is derived is to use aggregate statistics. For example, there is a fairly close statistical correlation between disposable personal income and consumer spending for food (see Exhibit 19). There is also a fairly close correlation between the sales of gasoline and the rate of new car registrations. Thus, if the reader were to assume that he were engaged in the manufacture of a basic food product, and also assuming that the growth of disposable per-

EXHIBIT 20   Life Cycle Worksheet

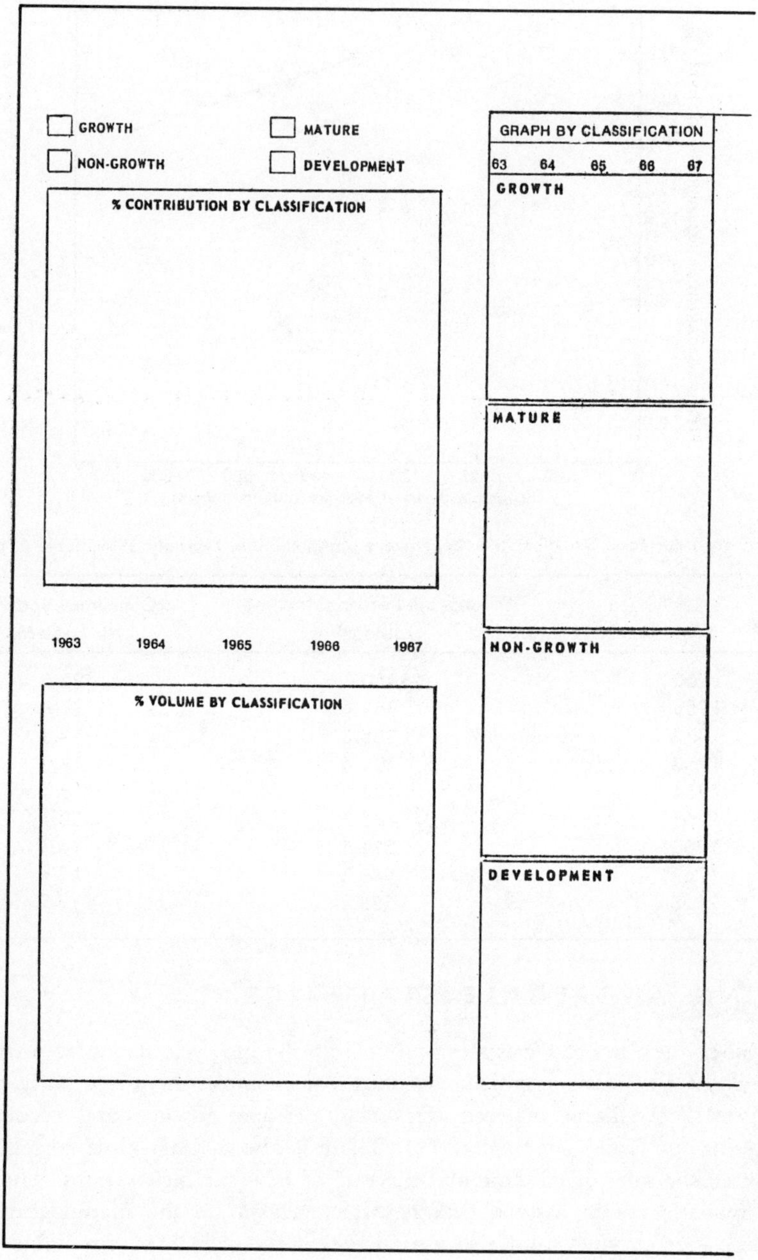

☐ GROWTH   ☐ MATURE

☐ NON-GROWTH   ☐ DEVELOPMENT

% CONTRIBUTION BY CLASSIFICATION

1963   1964   1965   1966   1967

% VOLUME BY CLASSIFICATION

GRAPH BY CLASSIFICATION

63   64   65   66   67

GROWTH

MATURE

NON-GROWTH

DEVELOPMENT

LIFE CYCLE WORKSHEET

PRODUCT BY CLASSIFICATION	COMPOUND GROWTH RATE	DIRECT PRODUCT PROFIT					VOLUME (000'S)				
		1963	1964	1965	1966	1967	1963	1964	1965	1966	1967
TOTAL											
TOTAL											
TOTAL											
TOTAL											

sonal income was about 3½% a year, it would be logical for the reader to reason that his product would be a growth product if the volume of his product exceeded a rate of growth in volume of 3½%. Likewise, an assumption might be made that his product was a mature product if its growth paralleled the rate of increase of consumer disposable income. Further, he might consider his product as a declining product if its growth did not match the rise in disposable personal income. This of course, is only one simplified way of establishing the source of profit expressed in terms of life cycle stages.

ANALYZING MARKETING EXPENDITURES

Another vehicle might be through the route of analyzing marketing expenditures and rate per unit of marketing expenditures over the life of a product. Other methods might include the stability of market share or, in the last analysis, simple intuition and observation. An additional vehicle that might be used to analyze marketing expenditures and segregate the characteristics of a product's performance into the stages of its life cycle, could be through the use of empirical observations based on the conclusions reached in the Mickwitz study referred to earlier. Statistical methods are available which would permit an examination of the intensity of various external factors such as advertising, quality, price, or service on a product's performance. Based on the relative intensity of these factors, it is possible to separate product characteristics into life cycle stages based upon the intensity of the various external factors.

Exhibit 20 is an illustration of a basic worksheet[17] to enable the reader to gain an insight into a technique which might be used to evaluate the quality and the risk inherent in profit.

SUMMARY

Thus far in our discussion of product life cycles and the relationship to the profitability of products, we have examined the concept of product life cycles as well as pertinent recent data which have been made available. The data suggest that the life of an average product is extremely short and, furthermore, that its performance is apparently limited to a brief number of recycling efforts. The implication of all of this data shows the importance of attempting to take the discretion of product life cycles out of the realm of theory and placing it into the practical marketplace where its importance can be evaluated and techniques devised to take advantage of its worth.

---

[17] Exhibit 20, Life Cycle Worksheet, was reproduced from a worksheet that originally appeared in an article written by this author in the June 1967 issue of *Financial Executive,* titled "Improved Marketing Analysis of Profitability, Relevant Costs, and Life Cycles."

5

Relating Product Life Cycle Analysis to Profitability Analysis

EVALUATING ALTERNATIVE PROFIT STRATEGIES

The last chapter laid the groundwork for the analysis that follows. The following discussion is based on a hypothetical situation in which a corporation is faced with the submission of two alternative marketing strategies. Each of the marketing strategies encompasses a vast product line and is in the form of a long-range plan.

Assume that Company Alpha has a product line which ranges from product A to product Q and that, further, it has arrived at a point in time where the annual marketing plan which covers the current year and the subsequent four years has been developed. In addition to the regular marketing plan which is called Plan A, an alternative plan, Plan B, has also been developed. The basic profit and volume data in each of the plans is shown in Exhibits 21 and 22.

The reader should notice that the concept of direct profit which was referred to in Chapter 2 is carried over into this analysis. One of the key operating highlights shown in Exhibits 21 and 22 is the profitability of the product expressed in terms of direct profit. The reader will recall that direct profit is that level of profit which is directly attributable to the existence of the product. *It is not* the marginal profit accruing from the product but rather the total profit which would not exist if the product did not exist. Essentially the summary of product performance shows an incremental picture of the prospects for each product as they are contained in the profit plan. The operating highlights, as presented for input purposes, do not include any allocations of corporate activities which already exist. To do this would defeat the purpose of presenting an incremental, or an out-of-pocket, look at the projections for each product.

In looking at Exhibits 21 and 22 note that the performance characteristics of product G show a precipitous increase in 1969 compared to 1968 but suddenly drop off dramatically in 1970 and then disappears from view altogether. Notice the different volume performances of the products in Plan A as opposed to the alternative Plan B. Plan A envisions a weaker performance, volume-wise, for Product B over the terms of the plan. Its volume is expected to increase from 65 million units to 80 million over the life of Plan A. In contrast, in Plan B, it is expected to achieve a volume of 81 million units by the end of the plan period. Product D, under Plan A, is expected to achieve a stronger sales performance over the terms of the plan than it is expected to achieve under the alternative of Plan B. Plan A calls for sales of one-half million more units over the plan period. One of the more dramatic differences between the plans is the stretching out of the demise of Product G in Plan B as contrasted with Plan A. The former envisions a stretching-out period of four years whereas Plan A envisions a demise for the product which will span a period of three years. A major influence in the profit plan is the acceleration of volume growth in Plan B for Product J. The interesting contrast to note is that whereas the end of the plan period in Plan B envisions a volume level of 19½ million units with a direct profit produced of $5 million, Plan A envisions a lower level of volume attainment (15 million units) but a higher level of direct profit ($6.2 million). This seeming contradiction can come about when a product is in its obsolescent or declining stage and the company marketing policy begins to take the shape of the one alluded to earlier in the text, wherein advertising and promotional investment for such products is held to a minimum until the product is allowed to find its sustaining volume levels.

Exhibits 23 and 24 build up the concept of life cycle segregation by summarizing some hypothesized product types together with the relevant basis for comparison of each product type. The growth rate of the base to be measured is shown along with the average annual growth rate of the product

EXHIBIT 21   Company Alpha—Marketing Plan, Plan A (1968 to 1972)

Product	Direct Profit (Thousands of Dollars)					Volume (Thousands of Units)				
	1968	1969	1970	1971	1972	1968	1969	1970	1971	1972
A	5,200	5,000	5,500	7,500	7,500	40,100	43,100	45,000	47,000	49,000
B	6,600	5,000	6,000	7,000	9,000	65,000	67,000	70,000	76,000	80,000
C	1,500	2,000	2,900	3,800	4,200	1,400	1,600	2,100	2,400	2,800
D	700	1,000	1,200	1,500	1,700	7,500	9,000	10,000	11,000	12,000
E	1,500	850	1,400	2,000	3,000	350	400	550	600	600
F	300	700	900	1,500	1,800	1,600	1,900	2,500	3,400	3,800
G	50	150	(1,600)	—	—	7,000	15,500	7,000	—	—
H	3,000	4,000	3,500	5,000	5,000	31,500	28,000	29,000	34,000	31,200
J	9,000	10,000	6,500	7,000	6,200	22,000	20,000	18,000	17,000	15,000
K	350	400	50	350	250	5,000	6,600	4,000	4,000	3,000
L	1,500	2,500	1,500	1,100	1,200	2,800	2,800	2,600	2,300	2,100
M	1,500	1,300	800	1,200	1,400	11,000	11,000	14,000	16,000	18,000
N	100	50	50	300	50	1,100	1,100	1,100	1,700	1,100
O	—	—	(100)	(50)	(50)	—	—	200	200	900
P	—	—	50	250	650	—	—	400	700	1,700
Q	—	—	—	(600)	(2,000)	—	—	—	100	1,500

EXHIBIT 22   Company Alpha—Marketing Plan, Plan B (1968 to 1972)

Product	Direct Profit (Thousands of Dollars)					Volume (Thousands of Units)				
	1968	1969	1970	1971	1972	1968	1969	1970	1971	1972
A	5,000	5,000	5,500	6,300	8,500	40,000	43,100	45,000	46,100	49,000
B	6,600	5,000	6,300	6,800	9,500	65,000	67,000	70,500	76,500	81,000
C	1,500	2,000	3,200	4,000	4,200	1,400	1,700	2,100	2,400	2,900
D	700	1,000	900	1,200	1,500	7,500	9,000	9,000	10,000	11,500
E	1,500	800	1,200	1,300	1,400	350	400	450	500	500
F	300	700	1,100	1,500	1,800	1,600	1,900	2,850	3,400	3,800
G	47	400	(1,900)	(500)	—	7,000	15,400	8,000	5,000	—
H	3,500	4,000	3,800	5,200	5,200	31,000	28,000	30,000	34,000	31,200
J	9,000	11,000	8,000	6,500	5,000	22,000	21,000	20,500	20,000	19,500
K	350	400	50	350	250	5,000	6,600	4,000	4,000	3,000
L	1,500	2,600	1,500	1,000	1,100	2,800	2,850	2,600	2,200	2,000
M	1,500	1,450	1,700	1,900	2,100	11,000	11,100	12,000	13,000	14,000
N	100	50	50	100	50	1,100	1,100	1,100	1,700	800
O	—	—	(100)	(50)	50	—	—	200	200	900
P	—	—	50	300	700	—	—	400	800	1,600
Q	—	—	—	(600)	(2,000)	—	—	—	100	1,500

volume performance. Based upon those growth rates, products are classified into life cycle phases. Notice that this differs from the Nielsen approach which classified life cycle phases on the basis of market share measures.

In an attempt to portray real life situations in the example, the author has introduced some particular product problems which cause changes in the characteristics of their performance. For example, Product G in Exhibit 23 is the same product referred to earlier whose volume increased from 7 million units in 1968 to 15.5 million units in 1969, then dropped markedly back to 7 million units in 1970, and disappeared from sight altogether (Exhibit 24). This is a classic situation of a new product that comes on stream infused with massive amounts of marketing investments, only to find that there is not sufficient consumer demand to take the product away from the shelf after the pipelines have been filled. As a result, in this particular example, Product G has been discontinued after the year 1970. When the characteristic condition of the lack of consumer demand became apparent in 1969, the product was reclassified from a growth product to a nongrowth product. It might be well at this point for the reader to consider that even though these things nominally are apparent in a plan which deals with future action, it may still benefit the corporation to keep the product on stream as long as it returns at least a marginal contribution. Therefore, although the plan theoretically has been constructed in the year 1968 and is being looked at in the year 1968, the fact that a falling off of the product is foreseen in two years does not mean that one immediately makes the decision to drop the product from the line. There may be financial trade-offs involved regarding inventories, tax benefits, and write-offs.

From Exhibit 23 we see that Product M is anticipated to show very modest growth between 1968 and 1969 and, based upon that growth, has been classified a mature product. However, further marketing strategy envisions dramatic technological breakthroughs in the area of flavorings which will permit the product to substantially outpace the growth of the market itself. As a result, in those years the product has been reclassified as a growth product. It may be easiest for the reader to compare the movement of products by viewing Exhibits 25 and 26 in conjunction with Exhibit 23. Exhibits 25 and 26 are worksheets showing the product performances, segregated into life cycle stages. In these exhibits, it is clearly shown that Product N moves from the mature stage into the growth stage in the year 1970 and forward and, in addition, Product G clearly moves from the growth stage into the nongrowth stage in 1970. Exhibits 25 and 26 are summarized in terms of dollars in the first half of Exhibits 27, 28, and 29 under the heading "Unadjusted."

EXHIBIT 23   Product Life Cycle Planning Data, Plan A (1968 to 1972)

Product	Type	Growth Rate of Base (Average Annual %)	Product Growth (Average Annual %)	Life Cycle Classification
A	Cocoa powder	1.0	5.6	Growth
B	Instant coffee	1.5	6.1	Growth
C	Instant tea	10.0	25.0	Growth
D	Ground coffee	3.0	15.0	Growth
E	Sugar syrups	11.0	10.7	Mature
F	Dessert topping	13.0	34.5	Growth
G	Frozen juice	—	—	Growth/nongrowth
H	Bread	1.5	(0.3)	Nongrowth
J	Laundry starch	1.0	(8.0)	Nongrowth
K	Blueing agents	2.0	(10.0)	Nongrowth
L	Milk shakes	1.0	(6.2)	Nongrowth
M	Gelatins	0.5	0.1/21.0	Mature/Growth
N	Margarines	0.5	—	Mature
O	Artificial sweeteners	—	—	Development
P	Frozen entrees	—	—	Development
Q	Paper specialties	—	—	Development

Relevant Base:
A Milk additives
B Instant coffee
C Instant tea
D Ground coffee
E Syrups
F Dessert toppings
G Retail beverage market
H Population growth
J Laundry aids
K Laundry aids
L Milk additives
M Gelatins
N Table spreads
O Sweetening agents
P Frozen foods
Q Retail paper products

EXHIBIT 24 Product Life Cycle Planning Data, Plan B (1968 to 1972)

Product	Type	Relevant Base	Growth Rate of Base (Average Annual %)	Product Growth (Average Annual %)	Life Cycle Classification
A	Cocoa powder	Milk additives	1.0	5.6	Growth
B	Instant coffee	Instant coffee	1.5	6.1	Growth
C	Instant tea	Instant tea	10.0	26.8	Growth
D	Ground coffee	Ground coffee	3.0	15.3	Growth
E	Sugar syrups	Syrups	11.0	10.7	Mature
F	Dessert topping	Dessert toppings	13.0	34.5	Growth
G	Frozen juice	Retail beverage markets	—	—	Growth/nongrowth
H	Bread	Population growth	1.5	—	Nongrowth
J	Laundry starch	Laundry aids	1.0	(2.9)	Nongrowth
K	Blueing agents	Laundry aids	(2.0)	(10.0)	Nongrowth
L	Milk shakes	Milk additives	1.0	(7.1)	Nongrowth
M	Gelatins	Gelatin desserts	0.5	6.8	Mature
N	Margarines	Table spreads	0.5	(6.8)	Nongrowth
O	Artificial sweeteners	Sweetening agents	—	—	Development
P	Frozen entrees	Frozen foods	—	—	Development
Q	Paper specialties	Retail paper products	—	—	Development

EXHIBIT 25   Product Life Cycle Summary (Plan A)

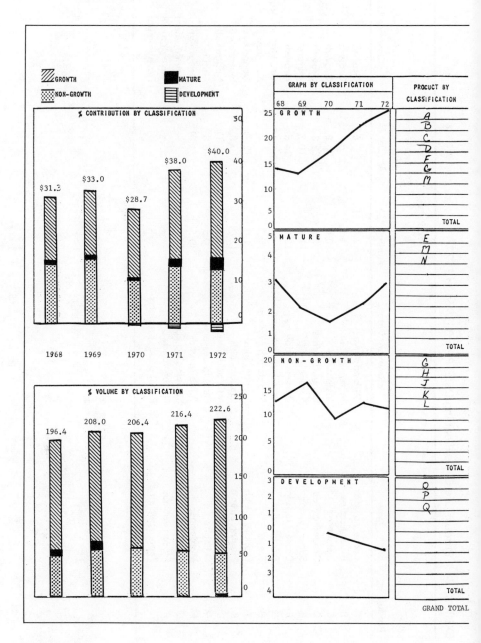

PLAN A

AVERAGE ANNUAL GROWTH RATE	DIRECT PRODUCT CONTRIBUTION					VOLUME (000'S)				
	F 1968	F 1969	F 1970	F 1971	F 1972	F 1968	F 1969	F 1970	F 1971	F 1972
5.6 %	5200	5000	5500	7500	7500	40100	43100	45000	47000	49000
6.1	6600	5000	6000	7000	9000	65000	67000	70000	76000	80000
25.0	1500	2000	2900	3800	4200	1400	1600	2100	2400	2800
15.0	700	1000	1200	1500	1700	7500	9000	10000	11000	12000
34.5	300	700	900	1500	1800	1600	1900	2500	3400	3800
-	50	150	-	-	-	7000	15500	-	-	-
21.0	-	-	800	1200	1400	-	-	14000	16000	18000
	14350	13850	17300	22500	25600	122600	138100	143600	155800	165600
10.7	1500	850	1400	2000	3000	350	400	550	600	500
.1	1500	1300	-	-	-	11000	11000	-	-	-
-	100	50	50	300	50	1100	1100	1100	1700	1100
	3100	2200	1450	2300	3050	12450	12500	1650	2300	1600
-	-	-	(1600)			-	-	7000		
(.3)	3000	4000	3500	5000	5000	31500	28000	29000	34000	31200
(8.0)	9000	10000	6500	7000	6200	22000	20000	18000	17000	15000
(10.0)	350	400	50	350	250	5000	6600	4000	4000	3000
(6.2)	1500	2500	1500	1100	1200	2800	2800	2600	2300	2100
	13850	16900	9950	13450	12650	61300	57400	60600	57300	51300
-	-	-	(100)	(50)	50	-	-	200	200	900
-	-	-	50	350	650	-	-	400	700	1700
-	-	-	-	(600)	(2000)	-	-	-	100	1500
			(50)	(300)	(1300)	-	-	600	1000	4100
	31300	32950	28650	37750	40000	196350	208000	206450	216400	222600

101

EXHIBIT 26   Product Life Cycle Summary (Plan B)

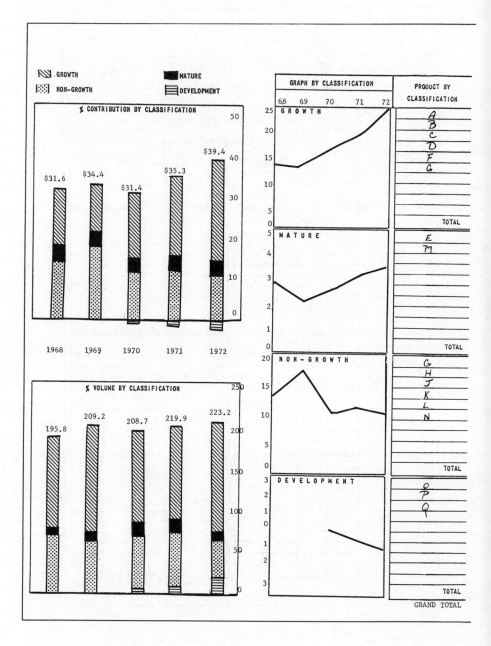

AVERAGE ANNUAL GROWTH RATE	DIRECT PRODUCT CONTRIBUTION					VOLUME (000'S)				
	F 1968	F 1969	F 1970	F 1971	F 1972	F 1968	F 1969	F 1970	F 1971	F 1972
5.6 %	5000	5000	5500	6300	8500	40000	43100	45000	46100	49000
6.1	6600	5000	6300	6800	9500	65000	67000	70500	76500	81000
26.8	1500	2000	3200	4000	4200	1400	1700	2100	2400	2900
15.3	700	1000	900	1200	1500	7500	9000	9000	10000	11500
34.5	300	700	1100	1500	1800	1600	1900	2850	3400	3800
—	47	400	—	—	—	7000	15400	—	—	—
	14147	14100	17000	19800	25500	122500	138100	129450	138400	148200
10.7	1500	800	1200	1300	1400	350	400	450	500	500
6.8	1500	1450	1700	1900	2100	11000	11100	12000	13000	14000
	3000	2250	2900	3200	3500	11350	11500	12450	13500	14500
—			(1900)	(500)	—			8000	5000	
—	3500	4000	3800	5200	5200	31000	28000	31000	34100	31200
(2.9)	9000	11000	8000	6500	5000	22000	21000	20500	20000	19500
(10.0)	350	400	50	350	250	5000	6600	4000	4000	3000
(7.1)	1500	2600	1500	1000	1100	2800	2850	2600	2200	2000
(6.8)	100	50	50	100	50	1100	1100	1100	1700	800
	14450	18050	11500	12650	11600	61900	59550	66200	66900	56500
—	—	—	(100)	(50)	50	—	—	200	200	900
—	—	—	50	300	700	—	—	400	800	1600
—	—	—		(600)	(2000)	—	—	—	100	1500
	—	—	(50)	(350)	(1250)	—	—	600	1100	4000
	31597	34400	31350	35300	39350	195750	209150	208700	219900	223200

The essential steps that are necessary in order to apply the analysis of the sources of profit through the profitability concept itself are as follows.

1. Establish the plan input such as shown in Exhibits 21 and 22 on a suitable worksheet somewhat resembling the example given in Exhibit 20.

2. Establish the growth rate for the base against which individual product will be measured and compare that growth rate with the growth rate of the product itself.

3. Based on the acceleration shown in the growth rates, classify products into the stages of the life cycle.

4. Record products on the Exhibit 20 worksheet in the upper segment of that statement in the section appropriate to their proper life cycle stages.

5. Arithmetically add, by year, the direct profit and the volume by the product for each life cycle classification.

6. Apply the quality factors as shown in Exhibits 27 and 28.

7. Compare the results of the alternative plans on an "Adjusted" basis as shown in Exhibit 29.

It is clear that on an "Unadjusted" basis, alternative Plan B is superior in terms of incremental direct profit dollars than Plan A over the time horizon of the profit plan. This is evident by comparing the $172 million return with the $170.8 million return for Plan A. Up to this stage of the

EXHIBIT 27 Summary Results, Plan A (Thousands of Dollars)

	1968	1969	1970	1971	1972	Quality Factor
Unadjusted						
Growth	$14,350	$13,850	$17,300	$22,500	$25,600	
Mature	3,100	2,200	1,450	2,300	3,050	
Nongrowth	13,850	16,900	9,950	13,450	12,650	
Development	–	–	(50)	(400)	(1,300)	
Total	$31,300	$32,950	$28,650	$37,850	$40,000	
Adjusted						
Growth	$28,700	$27,700	$34,600	$45,000	$51,200	2
Mature	3,100	2,200	1,450	2,300	3,050	1
Nongrowth	6,925	8,450	4,975	6,725	6,325	0.5
Development	–	–	(70)	(560)	(1,820)	1.4
Total	$38,725	$38,350	$40,955	$53,465	$58,755	

EXHIBIT 28   Summary Results, Plan B (Thousands of Dollars)

	1968	1969	1970	1971	1972	Quality Factor
Unadjusted						
Growth	$14,147	$14,100	$17,000	$19,800	$25,500	
Mature	3,000	2,250	2,900	3,200	3,500	
Nongrowth	14,450	18,050	11,500	12,650	11,600	
Development	–	–	(50)	(350)	(1,250)	
Total	$31,597	$34,400	$31,350	$35,300	$39,350	
Adjusted						
Growth	$28,294	$28,200	$34,000	$39,600	$51,000	2
Mature	3,000	2,250	2,900	3,200	3,500	1
Nongrowth	7,225	9,025	5,750	6,325	5,800	0.5
Development	–	–	(70)	(490)	(1,750)	1.4
Total	$38,519	$39,475	$42,580	$48,635	$58,550	

EXHIBIT 29   Comparison of Alternative Plan Results (Thousands of Dollars)

Year	Plan A	Plan B
Unadjusted		
1968	$ 31,300	$ 31,597
1969	32,950	34,400
1970	28,650	31,350
1971	37,850	35,300
1972	40,000	39,350
Total	$170,750	$171,997
Adjusted		
1968	$ 38,725	$ 38,519
1969	38,350	39,475
1970	40,955	42,580
1971	53,465	48,635
1972	58,755	58,550
Total	$230,250	$227,759

analysis, the incremental profits contained in the profit plan for the product line have been isolated into life cycle stages, and the dollar aggregates for profits from each stage have been summarized without regard to the quality of those dollars or the risk involved in achieving these dollars. Without going into long detailed explanations of the cost of capital, the author would simply like to refer at this point to the implications of the life cycle theory. In the following discussion, the cost of capital, as defined, will be considered as the minimum cutoff rate for capital projects or the target rate of return.

The factor of quality, which is the next process in the step of analysis to be introduced, is necessarily an intuitive one of the cost of capital. As an example, many companies distinguish between the target rate of return which they require for capital projects dealing with new products as opposed to those dealing with established products or simply cost reduction projects. In effect, a premium is demanded for the newness of products reflecting the greater risk involved.

For purposes of the example shown, assume that the dollars of profit derived from a mature product will be the established base from which all other dollars will be measured. It can reasonably be hypothesized that the dollar of profit derived from growth products with a foreseeably longer stream of earning potential are worth more than twice as much as those derived from mature products. Therefore, the factor assigned to the growth stage of a product life cycle will be the factor two, whereas the factor assigned to mature products will be the factor one. Dollars of profit when derived from products considered to be in the nongrowth stage are, of course, worth less than those derived from mature products. For purposes of this example, let us assume that the factor to be applied for nongrowth products is .5, in effect saying that the dollar of profit measured in comparative terms is really worth only 50¢ when it is derived from a nongrowth product. Developmental products, on the other hand, are products which will realize losses initially but which have a great potential for either growing and evolving into the growth stage or of being dropped altogether. For purposes of this example, the author has assigned a factor of 1.4 to developmental products. This says, in effect, that because there is the potential to achieve profitability the dollar of profit which may be derived from a developmental product is worth $1.40 in comparison to that derived from the mature product. Conversely, the loss in the event that the product will not reach fruition or mass marketing has an impact on the company equal to $1.40 as opposed to $1.00 for any type of mature product.

These factors are arbitrary and they can be argued. Whether the factors are absolutely correct though is irrelevant to the technique of analysis being used since the same factors will be applied to the analysis of both Plans A and B, therefore negating the impact of any changes in the factors, and will be measured on the basis of their intrinsic worth and not the mix of the factors. The lower portion of Exhibits 27, 28, and 29 show the transition from the unadjusted results for Plan A and Plan B to the adjusted results weighted by the quality factors. On a quality weighted basis, therefore, Exhibit 27 clearly shows that Plan A holds significant advantages over alternative Plan B. This advantage is in the magnitude of $2.5 million, whereas on an unadjusted basis, Plan B was shown to be superior.

SUMMARY

All of the foregoing discussion in the chapter and the example is intended to sensitize the reader to the impact of product life cycles and the utility of product life cycle planning in the marketing of products. There is a great deal of work still to be done in the development of this concept of product life cycle planning. At this stage it appears that the analysis techniques can easily be subject to statistical model building and correlation techniques. However, as yet, this has not been accomplished. Throughout all of the foregoing, the reader is cautioned to always use the rule of reason. It is too easy to create conclusions which appear to be sacrosanct because the conclusions were forced by numbers or statistical techniques. *Life cycle analysis has an exciting future* and the author is confident that just as the ideas which lay behind market segmentation have produced dramatic changes on marketing efforts, application of life cycle techniques and planning make the entire marketing process throughout the country more efficient.

CHAPTER | 6

The Return on
Investment Concept
and Acquisition Analysis

THE MEANING OF RETURN ON INVESTMENT

The abstraction of measuring what one receives in return for what one gives—the return on investment—has been in use professionally for almost three quarters of a century. Throughout this period, the ROI concept, just like the present value concept, has undergone periods of fads and times when the idea was so pregnant with possibilities that it became popular to improvise around its uses and assign to it glamorous terminology.

That an abstraction almost 75 years old can have a mystique which gives it waves of popularity is, after all, truly remarkable. In essence it is only a refinement of intuitive logic. In some respects, it is analogous to the process of creating detailed step-by-step procedures and timetables to accomplish an objective. This process of creating step-by-step procedures has been dressed up in modern terminology and now it is no longer the detailed process of logic but something called the critical path method (CPM), which carries with it an aura making it far less comprehensible to the observer who was reasonably familiar with the logic under its former folksy name.

The term, return on investment, means many things to many people. To the stockholder, the investment that is being measured is the stockholder's out-of-pocket expense in purchasing stocks. His return on that investment may be in the nature of the dividends which he receives or in the capital gains which he may earn on that investment. To the securities analyst, return on investment may mean the net profit after taxes for a corporation, measured in relation to the total equity of the corporation. To the internal manager, the return on investment may mean the operating profit of a division, measured against the assets employed within the division. To the product manager, it may mean the profitability of his product measured against the resources tied up by his product. Other operating managers may be concerned with the profit of segments within the company, measured against the resources in the form of assets employed by the company but excluding intangible items such as goodwill or amortization of patent rights. The latter two items are not physical expenses in an operating sense but rather represent a residue from an original commitment. As such, this type of expense does not affect current operating efficiencies. The most important fact to keep in mind, though, is that the return on investment measure is essentially a measure of finance. It is a quantitative tool that is rooted in accounting statistics.

From a strategic point of view, the return on investment concept is an essential link in meaningful decision-making. It provides the avenue by which alternative strategies can be measured and optimized and it also provides the decision-maker with a framework of reference against which past and future performances can be compared.

Profit does not exist in a vacuum; it must be supported by resources. When one speaks of the return on investment concept we are really speaking of the return on funds and funds are things of economic value. Like the term "profitability" which is also an elusive concept, ROI is a flexible tool which can be adapted and shaped to fill specific needs.

PROBLEMS ENCOUNTERED IN USING THE CONCEPT

The major problem inhibiting the creative use of the return on investment concept is that the phrase, having achieved popularity, has almost become generic and is no longer defined by its users. Because there are innumerable variations of profit levels, a proper question, initially, is *what return* is being used for the measure? Examples of profit levels, for instance, are profit before taxes, operating profit, direct profit, profit after taxes, cash flow, division profit contribution, factory contribution, or geographic contribution. Any of these profit levels are useful measures, depending on the investment base which is being employed.

An equally important question is *what investment?* It may be total parent company investment, the total investment of subsidiaries, total assets, manipulative assets (excluding intangibles), funds employed (tangible working capital), or selected bases (receivables, inventories, cash, etc.). The remaining question is *whose investment?* The investment of the stockholder differs in concept with the operating investment viewed from the eyes of the firm. The use of each may give startlingly different results, especially in the case where tangible funds employed in the firm are contrasted with the stockholder's investment in that same firm if large amounts of goodwill are capitalized.

Essentially, the concept of return on investment measures the efficiency of profits rather than profit dollars which can tend to be misleading during periods of inflation or deflation. The use of the concept can eliminate, in part, the effect of changes in price levels. It will also enable the user to compare current performance against either a historical performance or a standard return. Moreover, decision-makers can determine the optimum investment avenues for funds and, in addition, it is an especially useful technique for the evaluation of new products and capital investments.

The computation of the return on investment is, however, only part of the entire process of planning and control. To provide the most effective measure of performance, the actual return must be measured against some standard of performance which is fixed and is considered an attainable corporate, divisional, or profit goal. *In this chapter, it is suggested that the cost of capital be considered as the minimum acceptable return on investment for a corporation.*

Throughout the years, most of our great corporations grew by the seat of their manager's pants. The expectations were that a reasonable return would be earned on the money placed in the business. Those managers who survived proved to be the skilled entrepreneurs. Their intuition was such that their sixth, seventh, and probably eighth senses led them in the right direction. We are all aware that today we are increasingly being given more tools to enable us to make decisions and, as a consequence, the seats of our pants are less shiny that those of our counterparts of 40 or even 30 years ago.

In an effort to compartmentalize and isolate the important factors of control and information in a business, managements have splintered the enterprise into subsidiaries or divisions or, even further, into cost centers. Theoretically, if one can measure the return on an entire business, the return on its segments should also be measurable. Unfortunately, measurements of these segments are still difficult and the effects of operations continue to be hard to determine. The basic cause of the difficulty is in assigning assets to the segments of a business. Corporations often face the "Hamlet" conundrum: to allocate or not to allocate. When they do allocate, as some must, they may face further problems.

A few years ago, *Business Week* had a feature article about the American Telephone and Telegraph Corporation which dealt with the then breaking problem of the FCC attempts to change, in effect, the rate-making structure of the company. AT&T is permitted under law to earn a stipulated return on corporate investment. A significant area of the current inquiry derives from the concern of the FCC with the mix of the various subsidiaries' returns.

A paragraph in that article says the FCC ordered an investigation into the revenue requirements of all Bell System companies, including the "reasonableness and propriety of procedures used in *allocating investment costs.*"

Another difficulty is the treatment of the subject in the academic world. Although incremental working capital requirements are alluded to in some texts, their importance is largely played down in illustrating practical approaches to ROI. Frequently, the time value of this item overshadows in importance the original investment itself. In addition to this, academicians have not reached agreement concerning the elusive concept of incremental future patterns of cost of capital. The problem is not so much one of measuring what the cost of capital has been as it is measuring what its configuration will be after a given decision has been effected. *As used in this chapter, cost of capital will also be considered as the minimum cutoff point for investments or as a target rate of return.*

THE COST OF CAPITAL

The problem with the concept is that there is little agreement about the configuration of the cost of capital curve. The controversy arose from broad application of mathematics which swept first through education, particularly education in corporate finance, and eventually through business.

The controversy began about twelve years ago with a paper delivered to the Econometric Society by Franco Modigliani and Merton Miller. The title of their presentation, "The Cost of Capital, Corporation Finance, and the Theory of Investment," was imposing enough to presage the furor it has generated. M & M, as they are affectionately called, theorized that stockholders are basically indifferent to the distinction between $1.00 derived from equity sales and $1.00 derived from debt. The framework of their theory was a perfect market in which all investors act rationally and in which companies can be segregated into classes of like risk. They took studies of oil companies and utilities and measured cost of capital and yields. In essence, they concluded that the average cost of capital had a flat configuration. In other words, the average cost of capital is independent of a firm's capital structure and is equal to the capitalization rate of a pure equity stream of its class. (The capitalization rate is the reciprocal of a price/earnings ratio expressed as a percentage.)

Their presentation brought the house down because it ran counter to traditional theory which held that as a company increased its leverage through tax-deductible debt borrowing, its cost-of-capital curve dipped until the point was reached where higher leverage implied increased risk in the eyes of the lenders. Normally, one would expect that as you borrow more the risk of nonpayment of debt becomes greater. This has been the traditional view in lending circles. However, in the perfect world of M & M no such phenomenon took place. An example of the traditional view of risk involved in borrowing as a result of large amounts of debts incurred might be easily seen in Table VI.

TABLE VI   The Ultra Company

Debt (%)	Equity (%)	Borrowing Rate (%)
10	90	Prime (6%)
20	80	Prime (6%)
30	70	6¼
40	60	6½
50	50	7

The publication of the M & M work precipitated a rash of replies by many theorists. The most lucid analysis and refutation of the M & M ideas was by Alexander Barges called "The Effect of Capital Structure on the Cost of Capital." It is important to keep in mind at this point that the use of the cost of capital number should be as a minimal acceptable rate for any investment. Table VII illustrates one of the methods by which the cost of capital rate can be computed.

The use of the amount calculated as the cost of capital rate is not an end in itself; it is only a springboard from which acceptability criteria should be created. Acceptability criteria are merely those guidelines which will help the decision-maker to decide what capital investments should be undertaken by his business. After all, not every proposal that comes forth will meet

TABLE VII   The Ultra Company (Millions of Dollars)

	Amount	Interest Rate	Weighted Cost
Long-term debt	$ 200	3%	$ 6
Preferred stock	50	6%	3
Common stock	800	10%	80
	$1,050		$89

$$\frac{89}{/1050} = 8.5\%$$

minimum acceptable criteria of the company. If the proposal does not at least return an amount equal to the cost of the proposal, it would tend to dilute the earnings per share of the company or, in accounting terminology, the equity. For example, one large company in its capital program classified products by different justifications. Projects that are justified primarily for cost reduction purposes are required to generate a return on investment over a 10-year period as low as 20%. This is acceptable provided the end product involved is believed to be a reasonably permanent part of the line and the facilities involved are so flexible that they may be useable for successor products. Another category of capital item for that same company deals with projects that are designed primarily to increase production capacity for an existing product. Now here we are entering into a slightly higher risk situation and, therefore, that same company requires that the project generate at least a 10-year return on investment of no less than 20%. The highest risk category, of course, includes those projects which are designed to provide facilities to manufacture and distribute a new product or product line. The required return on investment to be generated by such a project is not less than a 10-year return on investment of 40%. Each of the above return on investment requirements is calculated on a before tax basis.

Thus far in this chapter we have been concerned with the difficulties inherent in the application of the ROI concept. It is time now to elaborate on the positive side and illustrate the right things about the concept and develop workable techniques from which meaningful, practical results can be derived.

THE DISCOUNTED CASH FLOW TECHNIQUE

There will be no attempt here to restate all that has been written about return on investment. Indeed, probably too much has been written about comparing different time values with nontimed value techniques. In all of the following illustrations, the present value technique, known as discounted cash flow, will be used mainly because of the author's preference. The discounted cash flow technique takes future flows of income which will derive from an investment and discounts the future value of the money by a suitable interest rate so that its value today may be known. The interest rate that is chosen to be applied is one which is achieved through a trial-and-error method. From the point of view of logic, it tries to show the economic consequences of the risk involved and the foregoing of an investment opportunity involved in not receiving money for a period of time. In other words, if you had the opportunity now to invest money at 14% and someone came to you and indicated that they would rather give you money 10 years from now, it would be obvious to you that the preferable avenue is to have the money now. Just how much money you would want to have now to equate to that dollar which would come years from now is the crux of the discounted cash flow calculation. In that particular instance, 26¢ in your pocket now, invested at 14%, would reach an accumulated total of $1.00, 10 years from now. This technique has the following advantages over the others.

1. It disciplines planning in that projects must be evaluated over a useful and reasonable life span.
2. It recognizes the time value of money.
3. Reinvestments are *not* assumed to be made at the cost of capital rate.
4. It avoids the fiction of computing in advance an exact cost of capital rate by using input data to find that rate.

The planning discipline which is required in the application of the discounted cash flow technique is far superior to that which is required in using the pure present value technique for evaluating projects and is certainly far superior to that used in calculating the payback period for capital projects. The term *payback period* refers to the length of time it takes for the accumulated cash flow from a project to equate with the accumulated investment in that project. *Cash flow* is accounting terminology for the net profit after taxes of a project, plus the noncash charges which were used in computing the net profit after taxes. These noncash charges may take the form of depreciation or amortization. Although they are valid economic and tax deductions, in order to reflect the operating earnings from a project, they nevertheless did not require any cash outlay, whereas other expenses such as labor and materials do require cash. The cash flow concept, therefore, is an attempt to define cash earnings accruing from an entity. Normally, calculations involving payback periods do not run over a span of five years. The balance of the useful life of the project is simply assumed away in the calculation. The only real virtue in using payback is that in applying the technique to a project which has a long, useful life, the reciprocal of the payback will quite often yield the approximate return on investment number when calculated under the discounted cash flow technique. Thus, a project which generated a payback in five years will probably generate a return on investment rate of approximately 20%. The virtue of recognizing the time value of money is too obvious to expand upon since, in these current inflationary times, it should be apparent to the wise businessman that a dollar in the pocket or in the bank now will earn an interest rate at least equivalent to offsetting the inflationary rate or the depreciation rate of the dollar. We are living in a time when it probably never made as much sense to borrow as it does now.

THE USE OF PRESENT VALUE AND PROFITABILITY

When using the conventional present value technique for evaluating the efficiency of capital investments, that technique will produce an answer expressed in terms of current value. Two pieces of input data are necessary in order to accomplish the calculation. The first piece of data which is required is a norm against which dollars of income flow will be measured. This rate normally is the cost of capital rate or some other appropriate rate which might be used, such as a target rate of return. A second factor is the dollars of cash inflow which will be derived from a project over a future period. The dollars of cash flow which will be earned are multiplied by the factors in each year that the cash flow comes in. These factors are the apppropriate ones computed for the base rate which is to be used as the norm. There are many preprinted tables giving this information. These results are compared to similar projects also undergoing consideration, and that project which has the highest amount of present value dollars is the one which nominally should be accepted. The distinction between that technique and the discounted cash flow as a technique is that discounted cash flow does not assume in advance an interest rate to be applied to the flow of income. Instead, the flows are compared with the initial investment in that project. Then, an *interest rate is sought* which will equate the investment (outflow) with the cash flow (inflow). The reader should note also that, in making caluculations under the discounted cash flow method, it is preferable not to apply any interest costs to the projects, since by introducing interest cost as a carrying charge for the project, it, in effect, counts the same interest twice in that criteria for the project itself is an interest rate.

Cash flow, then, computed for purposes of arriving at a return on investment calculation should be based upon profitability statistics, *excluding* the effect of interest either as an expense or in the taxes. This will be made clearer in exhibits later in the Chapter illustrating sample creative uses of the return on investment concept.

Most explanations of the use of ROI techniques deal with capital project analysis of possibly the creation of a new product. These are probably the most popular uses for the technique aside from aggregate corporate measures. This generalization is consonant with independent research recently completed by the writer and referred to earlier. One large company that was interviewed chooses not to motivate its division managers by using ROI goals because, with relatively small divisional investments and consequent high ROI, motivation becomes a meaningless numbers game of degrees. It is rather difficult to tell a division manager that last year the return on investment for his division was 35% and that this year it is expected that he will produce 36%. Each of the numbers is far higher than the average for American industry. Therefore, as a motivator, it loses its appeal. The particular company in question relies upon the tool of profit margin goal, rather than expressing its goals in terms of return on investment. Actually, their profit goals to the division managers are expressed in terms of earnings per share, broken down to the tenth of a cent level.

In the examples of problems which are shown in later portions of this chapter, various profit and investment levels are used, depending upon the type of answer which is required and type of problem which is being analyzed. It is important to keep in mind that when the reader sees the terms profit (return) or investment, there may be many different kinds of combinations which will satisfy the requirements of the problem. In all of the examples in this chapter, the profitability concepts set forth in the first three chapters will be employed. Thus, for the most part, direct profit will be a key number in the solution to all of the problems. However, the investment base against which the return is measured can be a variety of combinations. As an example, some companies use the concept of the return on funds employed or, expressed in a different manner, return on tangible assets capable of being manipulated by the firm.

FUNDS EMPLOYED

Funds employed consist of the following:

Cash
Accounts and notes receivable

Total inventories
Prepaid and deferred expenses
Miscellaneous investments
Long-term receivables
Net fixed assets
    Total assets
Less: Total current liabilities

In essence, the return is the relationship between the average funds employed and the profit produced by those funds. Another way of expressing the above composition of funds employed might be to call it tangible net worth. When using the return on funds employed approach, the author prefers that the funds employed for any year will be the average of the opening balance for the year, except for items such as cash and taxes, which are easier computed by means of a formula.

In other types of problems where incremental investments are being analyzed, the proper base for the computation of investment may consist only of net working capital, including accounts receivable and inventories.

EXHIBIT 30   The Return on Investment Cycle

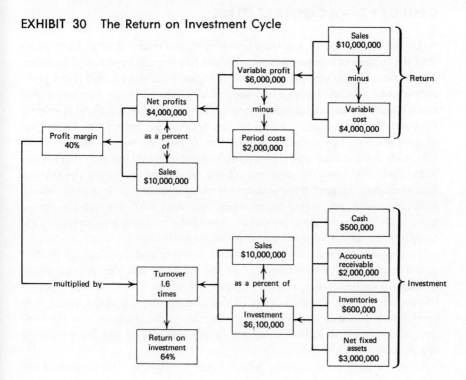

It may be easy for the reader to mentally visualize the tracing and composition of the return on investment concept by viewing Exhibit 30. That exhibit traces the final equation from its genesis in the concept of profitability and from the capitalization of the company.

There are many practical applications of ROI and the examples in this and subsequent chapters will deal with the following situations:

(a) Establishing a purchase price for an acquisition
(b) Capital project analysis and research and development
(c) Establishing a price for a product
(d) Evaluation of a market area
(e) Lease versus purchase decisions
(f) The evaluation of a marginal salesman
(g) Capitalization versus expense decisions

APPLICATIONS OF THE ROI CONCEPT—ACQUISITIONS

The author would be less than honest with the reader if he did not admit that the subject of mergers and acquisitions has literally been talked to death. At the time of this writing, it is mod, it's what's happening and there probably is not a prudent businessman around who is not in some way aware that there is such a word as "conglomerate." That the subject is current is evident by the fact that suddenly everyone has become an expert on the subject of acquisitions. The decision whether to acquire or not to acquire is an extremely complex one and the author does not seriously feel that there is one individual with complete expertise who is capable of mastering the subject. Unfortunately, most of the discussions dealing with acquisitions and, indeed, seminars which are taking place daily and deal with acquisitions devote most of their time to the quantitative side of the problem and inevitably get caught in the morass of pooling versus purchase arguments.

Techniques of profitability analysis on mergers and acquisitions encompass not only the quantitative side of the problem but also a great many qualitative factors which must be considered in the merger game. In order to properly present a capsule view of the merger and acquisition game, it is probably best to give the reader a perspective of the problem and the considerations involved in determining whether one should acquire or should not acquire.

When preparing the material which forms the basis for this portion of the chapter, the author, in order to ensure his immortality, invented a law of behavior, called Goodman's Law of Acquisitions. Simply stated, it says *that there is a 67% probability that the urge to merge will lead to a surge rather than a dirge.*

Sometime ago, a study was made by one of our leading management consultant companies and it concluded that slightly less than two-thirds of company acquisitions have proven satisfactory to the acquiring company. The main problems which emerge when one considers acquisitions probably revolve around the following main points, some of which were discussed in the study.

1. Companies who are aggressively acquisition-minded, such as conglomerates, lack marketing expertise. Very frequently the prime short-term considerations are financial. As a result, marketing efforts, which are essentially long-term strategy, become fragmented. Because marketing efforts are fragmented, many companies lack a unified marketing image. This year it is expected that conglomerates in particular will acquire companies whose assets are worth over $10 billion. More importantly, the acquiring companies are widely diverse in nature. As an example, RCA tried to acquire St. Regis Paper Company. An insurance company, The Insurance Company of North America (INA), desires to acquire an air line (World Airways). A financial company (Trans America) wants to take over a broadcasting company, Metro Media. Within these companies, there must be extensive marketing coordination extended down to subsidiary levels if these proposed mergers are to be successful. We already have evidence that many other conglomerates, which are not mentioned, are in trouble from a marketing point of view because they have tended to give unified advertising policies somewhat of a brushoff.

2. There is a failure on the part of the acquiring company to define exactly what business it is in. One highly successful company, Trans America, has defined what business it wants to be in and, briefly stated, it is the business of furnishing services to people at the lowest cost possible. This is an example of a company with a unity of purpose.

Some other companies who have achieved the unity of purpose can best be exemplified by Mohasco, a maker of carpets and furniture. It has stated that it regarded itself as a total supplier of home furnishings. Kinney National Services is predicated on a program of providing services for the public whether it involves car leasing, funeral parlors, or parking garages. Genesco likewise admits that they are a "total apparel" organization.

3. There is a lack on the part of the acquiring corporation to have an organizational philosophy or stated established objectives. In the previous discussion, mention was made of the definition of business on the part of the acquiring company. Pinpointing the objectives of a corporation is somewhat

similar to that except that here we are dealing with quantitative terms. For example, North American Rockwell Corporation has a target rate of return for annual growth of 10% or better in per share earnings and an average return of 15% or better on shareholder's equity. This is their objective. On the other hand, Trans America has an objective in earnings per share growth between 10 and 15% a year and a realization of 15% or more, after tax return on shareholder's equity.

4. A failure to place responsibility at a sufficiently high level within the acquiring corporation is a significant cause of mismanaged mergers. Conrad Jones of Booz-Allen-Hamilton once said that the biggest reason for flops is the failure of a company's chief executive to take an intense, direct, and continuing interest in the company that is being acquired. It is reasonable to hypothesize that the charting of growth within a corporation is the primary responsibility of the president. If there is one essential requirement for the job, this would by far be the most important aspect of the work of the corporate head. Most importantly, the participation in an acquisition or merger by the president does not stop once the company has been located and even after agreement has been consummated. It is probably at this point that the most important phase of the exercise of the president's responsibility should take place.

5. There is considerable reluctance to evaluate whether a potential acquisition will either buy or drain experienced people. Willard Rockwell, who is head of his own company, recently indicated in an article that making a merger work, in his view, is the art of taking over a company without overtaking. If the author had his druthers he would probably add that making a merger work is also the art of taking over people. One of the most important questions in any merger and acquisition negotiation is: Will the new combination result in increased management efficiency? Usually this is a particularly important question for the seller. The seller, of course, would want to assure himself that the buyer's management would be reasonably expected to remain employed in the capacity that it currently has for the foreseeable future. Morale-wise, it is unfortunate if people who are being acquired suddenly find themselves reporting to people other than those they expected.

A very prominent publishing firm in New York is having considerable problems of indigestion as a result of acquiring too many companies within too short a period of time. The companies that were acquired did not truly have the management capabilities within themselves to succeed. Although the company is continuing in an extensive acquisition program, it has virtually no one left who will be able to step in and staff these new companies. Internally, it has drained itself of people with good management potential. Probably the most striking failure of the firm's program is that it is not seeking companies who have strong management, nor does it appear that this is one of the aims of the acquisition program. At best, such a program which does not have an overriding consideration of either purchasing or providing a training cadre for good managers within the acquiring company will fail, or at least (I should say at best) can only result in buying time which will permit the development of management personnel within the companies being acquired.

6. There is a reluctance to inquire into the product life cycle stages of the company being purchased. It is fashionable to merge. There is often an emotional aspect to the program, which precludes the acquiring company from truly planning or analyzing the situation into which it is getting itself. The subject of product life cycles has been discussed in depth in Chapter 4 and, therefore, it would be inappropriate to repeat the same material even though it is in the context of an acquisition. The author is therefore suggesting in substance that in addition to looking at the aggregate earnings of a company in terms of the magnitude of its increase or decrease, it is just as incumbent upon the acquiring company to look at the earnings in terms of the maturity of its sources. Questions should be asked about the company being acquired. Does the company being purchased have one or two product lines which are in the mature stage of their life cycle? Does the income derive from products which have reached the saturation stage of the life cycle, carrying with it all of the onus of limited growth or limited lifetime?

7. There is quite often a lack of appreciation as to the degree of conservativeness of the accounting methods employed by the acquired company. As indicated in earlier chapters, profits can be manipulated or the direction guided by the controller through the employment of generally accepted accounting principles. All of the techniques of LIFO versus FIFO, capitalization versus expense, flow through of tax credits versus amortization of tax credits, and straight line depreciation versus accelerated depreciation fall under the aegis of generally accepted accounting principles and, for the most part, have been discussed earlier in the book. Yet, the combination employed by any one company can have a profound effect upon its earnings. Therefore, it is always incumbent upon any company interested in acquiring another company to restate the earnings of the acquired company in terms of the methods employed by the surviving company.

Within recent months, a rash of changes have been made by steel companies, whereby the companies have switched from accelerated depreciation to the use of straight line depreciation in order to improve their earnings per share for purposes of stockholder relations. The author is therefore suggesting that it is not simply enough to take the *pro forma* statements of the company to be acquired and consolidate them into the statements of the company which is acquiring. Each should be stated on the basis comparable to the conservatism employed by the survivor.

8. Not enough has been written about the impact on business combinations of union integration and consolidation. There is the potential of a momentous impact on business combinations which results from the combining of various labor unions in newly created combinations.

One of the major points which has arisen and demonstrated itself to be a shining problem is the fact that it may not be easy to get the Teamsters Union and the United Auto Workers to sit down and combine and be represented by one surviving company. Nor, may the Plumbers and Steamfitters Union wish to be associated with the Candy and Confectioners Union.

In a similar vein, another problem which presents itself is the merging of various pension plans with a huge variety of provisions for portability of vested interests. It is quite conceivable that if the acquired company had a pension and welfare plan which is superior relative to portability and vested interests from the plan which is held by the surviving company, then it may very well be that the surviving company will have to improve its own plan at a great cost, in terms of future and past benefits, when it really had no intentions of doing so prior to the acquisition.

9. Many companies which have really not considered being bought out by larger companies should, in fact, consider that it might be advantageous for them to take this route. Many medium-sized firms that may be interested in European operations or having European affiliates might well consider a merger with a larger company with international operations. It takes a great deal of effort to market in Europe. To associate itself with an international company that already has European franchises may very well benefit the acquired company. In addition to that, many companies which have traditionally been run by strong personalities may also well consider to be acquired. This is especially true in the cosmetics industry where the heads of companies are often of the breed which have distinct personalities and are considered to be mavericks in the marketing sense. The strength of these companies is in their leaders. The creativity of these companies is in their leaders. It may not be sufficient, however, for reasonable continuity in the event that something happens to the leader. One acquisition broker noted that there are a large number of companies in the cosmetics industry doing only $5 to $10 million a year in sales, yet their expenses were all very high. Most of the high expense ratio to sales occurs because the government insists that each of the companies maintain very rigid quality control of their products. It could be quite advantageous for many of these smaller firms to combine and substantially cut their period costs which result from quality

control, without sacrificing quality itself. That same observer noted that the textile industry is also in a somewhat similar situation.

CHARACTERISTICS OF SUCCESSFUL ACQUISITIONS

The foregoing discussion has been a capsule delineation of some of the major problems that have shown up as a result of the emphasis on acquisition activity. Despite these problems, many of which are formidable, an analysis of companies who have successful acquisition records reveals that there are certain characteristics which are common to almost all of the companies.

One of these characteristics concerns itself with an attitude of aggressiveness as opposed to an attitude of passivity. The idea is to go out and look for companies and look for them with a purpose. It is not enough to wait for them to come to you. If you wait for them to come to you the chances are good that they have already been passed over by another company who has been interested in them.

The second characteristic of successful acquisition policy has been that companies seek the product; products do not seek the company. Look for the product and then look for the company behind it and then evaluate the company.

The third characteristic of successful companies is that they are unashamed to size up their own company. They have been quite willing to look at themselves and ask themselves honestly, why should Company X prefer my bid over the bid of my competitor? What is it that make me more attractive to them than my competitor? In this way, they have been able to rationalize their movements, to sharpen and hone their own objectives and their offers.

Lastly, these companies have been unashamed to use the hard sell in selling their own company. It takes a pro to buy a company and when you have that pro, he will know who to contact and how to contact. Should it be through a third party? Should you employ a lawyer in order to make the contact or should you go to a professional marriage broker in order to make the contact? The pro will have sized up which type of payment will be most acceptable to the acquired company. He will know the degree to which there may be vested and strong stockholder sentiments within the acquired company. In short, the difference between the conduct of business during a potential acquisition and merger operation, unlike a conventional marketing operation for a product, is that the marketing operation is usually so vast and dispersed in scale that it can be done by a boy. It takes a man to consummate an acquisition.

DEFINING PURCHASE PRICE

There is a definite relationship between successful acquisitions and the establishment of a purchase price. The relationship is quite apparent when companies that have a history of successful acquisition policies negotiate with a prospective candidate for acquisition. The entire climate of the negotiations takes place with an air of confidence and it is rare that extreme differences regarding the purchase price arise. This is in contrast to some of the less successful acquisitions whereby tender offers from many companies are submitted and the prospective acquisition price undergoes a constant transition, often leading the original acquirer to raise its offer numerous times.

At this point it is probably wise if w elook at some of the caveats which lie behind the simple and apparently innocent phrase which is called "purchase price." It was said earlier that profits do not exist in a vacuum and that they must be supported by resources. One of these resources is working capital. Working capital is simply the cash, accounts receivable, the inventories, and so forth which are needed to conduct everyday business. The importance of this is sometimes felt in the manner in which companies have been acquired. It may be that if you have plans to expand the operations of a company which you have just acquired, you are going to have to inject huge amounts of working capital into the company initially and then, subsequently, in proportion to its growth. Sometimes these costs may be far beyond the net profit and the capital investment shown in your projections for the company, and the purchase price which is shown in your plans. This point is clearly demonstrated in Exhibits 31 and 32.

Another caveat which exists beyond the purchase price is the potential for physical relocation of facilities. It may be that you have acquired a company that has a plant in Kenosha, Wisconsin and that, further, has a reasonably tight labor market. If two of your major competitors also happen to be located in Kenosha, Wisconsin and expect to expand their plants considerably, it can only have the potential of creating a noose on an already tight labor supply in the market. This noose could potentially drive you out of business. In appraising the physical location of plants of companies you acquire, you will constantly have to be aware of the competition and what the plans are relative to the competition. Questions will have to be asked such as, is it reasonable to expect that they will grow faster than your own plant? What will be the effect on the labor supply? What is the degree of unionization of your competitor's plants in areas where you have just acquired physical facilities? Is there adequate rail and truck transportation available? Again, this is another point which lies beyond the simple concept of a purchase price. Furthermore, what about changes in distribution patterns?

I know of an extremely large food processing company which had offered to it a number of years ago, a medium-sized company which makes a very well-known bread. The food processing company decided not to acquire the bread company because it meant that rather than having its salesmen call on key and direct accounts in the fashion they had been, they would also have to go out and, in effect, be rack jobbers. It was for the same reason that this food company also rejected an opportunity to purchase a very successful greeting card company, simply because of the method by which the product had to be supplied. They recognized that the opportunities for business combinations also brought about changes in distribution patterns which may not have been consonant with their own aims.

Another aspect to acquisitions which lies beyond the simple-sounding concept of purchase price is the potential for the combination to become a vehicle to enter into an unrelated third industry, beyond the bounds of the merger which is being consummated. A fine example of this occurred when the AVCO Corporation entered the financial field several years ago by means of the acquisition of the Delta Acceptance Corporation. The acquisition of a financing company gave AVCO Corporation the assets by which it was able to increase its cash and its borrowing power and only last year, AVCO was able to acquire an insurance company, Paul Revere, through this move.

A caution beyond the scope of the purchase price is that of corporate image. The Ling-Temco-Voughts, the Littons, the North American Rockwells have gained their reputations by working with the acquired managements and adopting a posture of "from now on it is 'we,' not 'you' or 'us.' "

Proceeding just slightly further along the path which began with a delineation of common problems, a generalization of patterns enjoyed by successful companies, and the preceding discussion about caveats which lie beyond the purchase price, I would like to alter direction slightly and talk about questions of risk existing between parties in a merger or acquisition.

RISKS BETWEEN PARTIES

Stockholders of respective companies that are about to combine view the risks of the business marriage much in the same way as nervous parents view their offspring who are about to enter into a mixed marriage. It is incumbent upon each of the parties to identify and appraise potential risks. If I were to speak to you assuming that you were an ultimate buyer instead of seller, I would suggest that you, as buyer, attempt to leave the risks with the seller. One of the ways in which this can be done is by precisely defining the parameters of the transaction. If an area has a potential risk in the form of possible or contingent liabilities, then the acquisiton route should not include the acquisition of the equity. It should only include the purchase of the assets so that liabilities that can be ascribed to those assets will be limited. In addition, as a buyer, you (the reader) can secure your peace of mind by obtaining contractual warranties or guaranties from the parties. This is very common in the case of the validity of accounts receivables and possible undisclosed liabilities.

Lastly in the area of risk, there is a growing trend to tie an acquisition's final sales price to its future performance. It is much the same as a buyer placing a down payment on a company with an understanding that the pot gets bigger later on, providing that the seller's earnings reach a certain contractual level. One top marriage broker has noted that Litton Industries has used this method a number of times with considerable success. The sellers have all obtained more money than they otherwise would have obtained.

The author would also advance to you that you consider that there is an opportunity risk in accepting cash (that is, if you are the seller) as opposed to a nontaxable stock swap transaction. In terms of the seller's best interest, a sale of assets only or entire equity may be the optimum. If the deal is for cash, then you, the buyer, may want to purchase only the seller's assets. By doing that, you, as the buyer, could avoid any liabilities the seller may have, for example, taxes or lawsuits.

This of course may *not* be in the seller's best interest. If he sells only his assets, he will be hit with an immediate capital gains tax. However, you may also have a strong selling point in asking that the seller accept cash. By accepting cash now, he can put it to work immediately. Even the Fisher-Lorie studies of the stock market showed that if investors had held securities for the long term, they could have earned an average of 9% annually. That is quite a selling point to a man who has intentions of establishing trusts for children.

FIVE AVENUES OF REJECTION

The perils of merger and acquisition adventure have made evident five avenues that should be rejected by any company intending to pursue an acquisition policy.

1. Do not buy manufacturing capacity.
2. Do not buy market share.
3. Do not look for purchasing advantages.
4. Do not dilute the equity.

5. Do not go into a business via the merger route if you would go into the same business anyway without the acquisition.

Growth can be expensive this way and your growing pains can be more than psychosomatic. Before checking the merger route, study carefully your own internal opportunities to accomplish the same end.

USING RETURN ON INVESTMENT FOR ACQUISITION CALCULATIONS

The keystone, of course, in the merger arts lies in the concept of return on investment. Once a decision has been made to acquire or not to acquire, and if the next step is to have all "systems go," the financial evaluation is logically the decision rule at this stage of the investigation.

Companies can be acquired in many ways. The latest "in" thing to do is to issue convertible preferred stock containing a provision whereby the dividend rate keeps ahead of the conversion rate. Investors are thus discouraged from converting the issue into common stock and thereby diluting the equity. Some companies have even been bought for old-fashioned cash. Many companies choose to establish a multiple of earnings basis. In order to use this approach to determine the price of an acquisition, the buyer must first categorize the perspective acquisition in terms of its growth potential and then apply some multiple of earnings. The weakness in this approach is the need for a price earnings multiple because the multiple changes randomly with each stock trade. Early in 1968, many business marriages were put off or cancelled because of the drop in the market. The method is entirely dependent upon the vagaries of investor psychology. Another technique is to assign some premium over the book value or going value of the business.

Behind the threads of all acquisition methodology is the nagging problem of determining the correct price to pay for an acquisition. It is probably obvious to all of us that there is no one correct price. Like the word "cost," delineation of "price" depends upon the use to which it going to be put. However, some generalizations are proper.

There are flaws in all of the above techniques because they revert to the adequacy of an individual's intuition and judgment. A simpler beginning can be formulated if ground rules for financial projections are established.

Using the present value concept and responsible financial projections, the following might serve as an example of a real-life problem. Company Beta is in a marrying mood. It has had its eye on Company Alpha for some time and after careful analysis has decided to attempt to acquire Alpha. Beta's target return on investment is 14%. The company does not want to dilute that goal. The chief financial officer asks for a calculation of the maximum offer it can make to Alpha consistent with Beta's goal.

Just as the secret of success in grandmother's cooking was the mix of the ingredients, here too the important element is the data—its accuracy and relevance.

A profit projection is established, followed by an estimate of incremental working capital requirements. We can surmise that as the business grows further injections of working capital beyond the initial amount will be required. In this particular illustration, shown in Exhibits 31 and 32. it is assumed that working capital turns over six times. One of the most important elements in the solution of the problem is to note that the past is not dwelled upon. The financial consideration given for an acquisition should be related to the future performance of the company as it is included in the plans of the acquirer. In this illustration it is assumed that a reasonable expectation of sales growth would approximate 10% on an average annual basis. Based on the configuration of the profit and loss statement, including those expenses that can be expected to be eliminated as a result of the merger, profit after taxes is expected to approximate 6% of sales. Depreciation is included in the effect of profit after taxes. After an initial capital investment has been made by the acquirer, it will not have an appreciable effect on earnings since the initial capital investment will not need to be reinfused over the time horizon of this example.

The result of the profit and loss analysis shows that cash flow (profit after taxes plus depreciation) will increase from $2 million in 1967 to $4.5 million in 1976. At this point the reader should reason that the cash flow will not completely benefit the corporation since the incremental working capital requirements mentioned earlier will cause a drain on that cash flow. This is especially evident in the initial year of the takeover when the massive infusion of funds takes place. Following that initial infusion of funds the only additional funds which will be required to be pumped into Company Alpha will be those funds which are generated solely as a result of growth. Thus, the reader may mentally calculate that incremental working capital required in 1968 can be computed by multiplying the difference between the 1968 versus 1967 sales and multiplying that amount by 16.7% which is the equivalent of a turnover of six times. The net cash flow shown on the bottom line is the final determinant of funds which will be flowing into Company Beta as a result of the acquisition.

EXHIBIT 31   Company Alpha—Acquisition, Estimating Net Cash Flow (Thousands of Dollars)

	1967	1968	1969	1970	1971	1972	1973	1974	1975	1976
Net sales—10% average growth	$31,500	$34,700	$38,200	$42,000	$46,200	$50,800	$55,900	$61,500	$67,700	$74,500
Profit after taxes— 6%	1,890	2,082	2,292	2,520	2,772	3,048	3,354	3,690	4,062	4,470
Depreciation	138	168	120	100	95	90	85	80	75	70
Cash flow	2,028	2,250	2,412	2,620	2,867	3,138	3,439	3,770	4,137	4,540
Less: Incremental working capital (16.7% of incremental sales)	5,252	533	584	633	700	767	850	934	1,034	1,133
Net cash flow	$ (3,224)	$ 1,717	$ 1,828	$ 1,987	$ 2,167	$ 2,371	$ 2,589	$ 2,836	$ 3,103	$ 3,407

Exhibit 32 shows those same funds including the repayment of the working capital in the year 1976, the end of the time horizon. The funds are shown discounted at an interest rate of 14% in accordance with the desired target return for the company. On this basis, the answer as presented is $10.2 million. Expressed in other terms, it would indicate that Company Beta can pay *as high as* $10.2 million for Company Alpha and still maintain a position whereby their 14% ROI target will not be violated. The last point of note in this particular problem dealing with mergers and acquisitions has to do with the return of the working capital. When a technique such as discounted cash flow is used, a time horizon is assumed. It is as if the project has a limited life. We can assume in looking at this project that Company Alpha will live only from the year 1967 through the year 1976. Under the assumptions implict in this technique, at that time, the inventory, the receivables, and any other varities of working capital should reasonably be converted into cash and returned to the acquired company.

EXHIBIT 32   Company Alpha—Acquisition, Calculation of Purchase Price
(Thousands of Dollars)

	Net Cash Flow	Factor at 14%	Discounted Value
1967	$ (3,324)	0.9332	$ (3,101)
1968	1,717	0.8112	1,393
1969	1,828	0.7053	1,289
1970	1,987	0.6131	1,218
1971	2,167	0.5330	1,155
1972	2,371	0.4634	1,099
1973	2,589	0.4029	1,043
1974	2,836	0.3502	993
1975	3,103	0.3045	945
1976	3,407	0.2647	902
1976	12,420	0.2647	3,288 Return of working capital
Discounted purchase price at 14% ROI			$10,224

7

Using Return on Investment for Capital Projects and New Product Development

The name of the game is growth. The importance of new products to the growth of individual companies cannot be overemphasized. An idea of how the proliferation of new products helps the growth of a company can be shown by the fact that the Campbell Company, makers of Campbell Soups, at the end of World War II had a total of 27 products. At the present time, the number of products produced by the company has increased to approximately 400 items. It is true that some of the increase came from acquisitions of other companies; however, a good portion of the total results from the introduction of products that were unheard of 20 years ago. The giant Procter & Gamble stated that new products played a major role in doubling Procter & Gamble's sales between 1955 and 1965. The entire lesson of product life cycles almost mandates that a company plan in advance for the decay of existing products and have ample good quality products ready to step in on the line to compensate for those products which have either begun or are completing their saturation stage of the life cycle.

Living standards in all markets, whether domestic or international, are increasing and the consumer is apparently willing to innovate in his choice of products and his testing of new product concepts. The same Procter & Gamble is currently in a fight for its toothpaste life with Lever Brothers and Colgate Palmolive. It has been estimated that almost $50 million will be spent to create new products and revitalize old standbys in the toothpaste field. At stake is a market worth approximately $350 million annually. New toothpaste concepts that brought a cosmetic touch to a heretofore staid product have created an awareness on the part of the leaders that there is an approach that can be segmented directly to today's affluent and active youth. Market research estimates have concluded that between $80 and $90 million of the total market value for toothpaste is more concerned with the cosmetic effect of toothpaste than its actual ability to inhibit tooth decay.

As a result, the campaign costs about $25 million and attempts to ignore health claims regarding caries and emphasizes the cosmetic ability of the toothpaste to enhance the whitening of the enamel. As part of the interplay, Bristol Myers has dropped its conservative Ipana toothpaste, long a fixture on the market. With these many dollars at stake, each of these companies cannot afford to lose and yet some will lose. In a crash program at Colgate which took place between 1960 and 1963, Colgate which originally spent about $7 million on product research, increased its outlay to .$10 million in that span of time. Test marketing itself, separate and apart from product research, rose from $2 million to about $18 million in the same period.

WHY NEW PRODUCTS FAIL

There are many risks and rewards in the new product game. Any company that fails to create and successfully market new products faces a very probable loss of sales and market share. Roy Kelly, Vice President of the National Biscuit Company, said that "a static product line is under constant competitive or obsolescence pressure. New products are not only pleasant things to have; they are a must if we are going to retain our place, turnover, and prestige in the marketplace." The challenge in the new products game is to create better decision-making techniques—those which will minimize risk. The need for these techniques is very evident when one considers the reasons why new products fail. Periodically the National Industrial Conference Board surveys business opinions and experience. The response to their question as to why new products fail,[18] brought forth eight primary reasons for failure:

---

[18] *Why New Products Fail,* National Industrial Conference Board, October 1964, Vol. 1, No. 10.

1. Inadequate market analysis
2. Product defect
3. Higher costs than anticipated
4. Poor timing
5. Competition
6. Insufficient marketing effort
7. Inadequate sales force
8. Weakness in distribution

Approximately one-third of the respondents in the study indicated that the most important reason for the disappointing showing of new products within their companies was insufficient knowledge of the market or even misjudgment of the market. Demography, of course, is becoming an art. We have all been very conscious of market segmentation ever since Timex became successful in marketing lower price watches. Yet, we have not truly been able to develop fail-safe techniques for accurately gauging the market or gaining meaningful clues as to the nature of the market. We have not yet, despite the proliferation of information about consumer buying habits, been able to anticipate the consumer. Most importantly, we have not yet developed techniques by which effective test marketing can confirm intuitive results. Most of the studies at the University of Michigan conducted by George Katona have demonstrated that *as a variable, the consumer is highly unpredictable. Purchase preference seems to change with the winds of the economy.* Glaring examples of *inadequate market analysis* in the consumer products field are becoming more apparent.

Many companies produce powder to be mixed with milk and to create chocolate drinks. A new product effort, which simultaneously brought forth new products from both The Nestlé Company and the General Foods Corporation, involved thickening agents and taste agents which would produce the effect of drinking a milk shake. Both companies and others which subsequently entered the field injected massive amounts of investment spending into the products and, yet, it was the consumer in the final analysis who indicated that the product was not significantly improved over the basic chocolate drink and, on a per serving basis, was far too expensive to purchase.

A good many of the executives who responded to the NICB survey indicated that product defects which were discovered after the product was lauched were also a primary cause of failure. One industrial machinery executive indicated that the product which was produced and launched later proved not to be sufficiently rugged when it was actually placed into service.

Much in the same vein, another firm in the same industry indicated that it believes that the principle causes of failure were related to the quality of the objectives of the initial product which were laid down for product engineering and the lack of adequate performance and durability tests. The increasing intervention of the government in the problems concerning the automobile industry has made us all aware of many of the massive recall programs for new cars. This type of recall is, of course, very directly related to the same product defects that plague new product launchings. The reader may be aware of one of the major appliance manufacturers who has attempted to solve this problem by producing products with easily replaceable major components so that, in effect, the purchaser can become a do-it-yourself repair man. Interestingly, one of the replies of a chemical company executive indicated that "perhaps more extensive pilot plant manufacturing studies would have helped us to anticipate and therefore solve or avoid our subsequent commercial manufacturing problems." This very concept of the conflict between a pilot plant or in-business manufacturing facilities is the subject of the specific return on investment example shown in Exhibits 33 through 37.

COST FACTORS

When costs are higher than anticipated, any of a number of factors can be singled out as a cause. In many cases, initial estimates are not made on an in-business basis. That is, the estimates only for test market results are computed and these often do not give effect to the mass production economies or the application of the learning curve theory. Often, costs on an in-business basis would produce a much truer level of expense to be anticipated.

TIMING FACTORS

Another crucial factor in the analysis of why new products sometimes fail in the question of timing. For example, it may happen that a change in market conditions will take place between the birth of the product and its ultimate marketing. It may result with a product that is out of date before it is marketed. Probably one of the most famous, recent examples of such a situation was the introduction of the Edsel. Another kind of obsolescence that results from technology comes from the failure to market a new product in time to prevent inroads of a competitive product. It was just such a consideration that caused the makers of Fab Detergent to market the new Fab with Borax immediately, rather than going into test market. It is dangerous to take up too much time in the test market stage of a product's life. Quite often prolonging the test of a good product idea gives the competition time to react and either muffle your surprise or create a competitive edge through various marketing investment spending.

A recent example of this occurred early in 1966 when Ralston Purina's Van Camp Seafood Division began testing cat foods in cans numbered consecutively up to the number seven. This made it possible to offer cats a daily treat and made it easier for the pet owner to remember which day of the week and which can should be used. The test, which began early in 1966, was prolonged until August 1967 when Purina decided to make the program national. When they did go national, they found that Quaker Oats, by that time, had a full line of cat food in numbered cans, also national.

COMPETITIVE FACTORS

Competitive action can, of course, also be a great cause of new product failure. When too many manufacturers of the same new product attempt to make inroads into a market of defined size, it can only result in a massive economic waste unless the market itself is subject to enlargement. Ball-point pens are a fine example of this type of economic waste which took place in the early 1950s as the pens were being developed. The maturity of this new product concept has, of course, led to the idea of market segmentation with various ball-point pens sold for varying prices. One of the respondents to the survey by the National Industrial Conference Board said that "we experienced a product failure which is still fresh in our memory. Unanticipated competitive price action rendered our product completely uneconomic and thus, failure." Of course, there is another side of the coin too and that is, that it is possible for this needle of competitor's action to provide the developing company with a mixed blessing. According to the president of a metal stamping company, one of their products was pulled out of the market just short of its formal introduction. The company took this action because a competitor beat them in terms of timing. The competitor had such a miserable failure in attempting to reach the public to accept the item that the company which originally developed the item got cold feet and decided not to enter the market with the product.

Quite often, companies that are intuitively linked to the life cycle of their products feels that their bread-and-butter items, the established products, should always take precedent and, therefore they will commit an insufficient marketing effort to the development of new products. Even after a new product is marketed, companies will frequently not commit sufficient resources on the basis that there are many higher elements of risk involved in the new products program. One of the respondents to the NICB survey, food manufacturer, described his company's weaknesses as follows: "If we have any one cause for failure which stands out above all others, it is an unwillingness to commit to new product introduction ventures, the marketing resources that are required to compete in the current market."

DISTRIBUTION FACTORS

Lastly, many companies have weaknesses in distribution or in an inadequate complement for the sales force which also assists new products to fail. The position taken by many of the companies regarding their sales forces is that they have an unlimited capacity to sell. There appears to be an ego factor involved in the attitudes of the company. The assumption is that if an additional line is added to the line carried by the salesman, he will have sufficient time to go out and represent this new product. Frequently what is overlooked is that the very existence of the new product creates the unique situation in which a potential buyer must be educated and sold to the worth of the product. This will entail an increased effort on the part of the salesman. The key, therefore, depends on the individual's capacity to sell and his capacity to absorb a new line. A highly desirable approach to adding a new product line vis-à-vis the capacity of the sales force is for sales management to carefully analyze the call patterns of the various salesmen and the characteristics of the market segmentation at which the product is directed.

WASTE IN PRODUCT DEVELOPMENT

The advertising firm of Batten, Barton, Durstine & Osborn at one time has estimated that the waste in research and development efforts approximate 70%. This is an appalling figure when one considers the billions of dollars expended towards these efforts. The food industry alone spends approximately $160 million in new product research and development. If that number were applied to this effort, then the logical conclusion would indicate that the food industry is wasting over $100 million each year. If that wasted effort could only be reduced from 70% to 50%, the industry would realize a net relative savings of over $30 million annually. The food industry is a representative industry to which we should direct our attention. There are approximately 35,000 items represented in food stores. These include sizes, brands, flavors, and type of items, including the private label foodstuffs.

These items are offered by over 38 chains and supermarket warehouses during an average business day. Franklin Graf, an executive of the A. C. Nielsen Company, has indicated in a recent speech that the average number of items handled per store totalled about 5800. The relation of this number to new product development becomes glaringly apparent when one realizes' that in any given year approximately 5500 items of foodstuffs are discontinued by these food stores while, at the same time, they receive an infusion of over 7300 new items. This, of course, has resulted in a net increase in authorized items on the shelf. Obviously, unless the stores can create sky hooks and wall stretchers, either of a number of alternatives must happen. Shelf facings for existing products must be reduced or increased shelf space must made available. An example cited by Mr. Graf occurred in the baby foods line. There, the number of items offered totalled 266 in the year 1965. Only a year later, even though 23 items had been discontinued, a total of 38 new ones had been authorized to take their place, resulting in a net increase of 15 items. The attrition rate for the 7300 new items which were introduced in the year 1966 was exceptionally high. By the end of the year, only 649 or approximately 58% of the total remained in distribution a year later.

Although statistics between the A. C. Nielsen Company and Booz Allen and Hamilton differ, their import is the same. The Nielsen Company reports that of 78 new items presented for development within the developing companies, 59 were rejected outright, 19 were forwarded to a new products committee and, of that amount, 18 were accepted. On the other hand, Booz Allen and Hamilton reports that in their own survey of 58 new product ideas, approximately 8 were forwarded for initial business analysis, 4 went on further for developmental work, 3 finally succeeded in being test marketed, and only 2 were commercially successful. In comparison to the Nielsen figure of 58% batting average for successful products, the Booz Allen statistics reflects only a 30% rate of success.

An important conclusion reached by Mr. Graf of the Nielsen Company was that their study found evidence of what one buyer called at least unprofessional selling at the chain level. Their remarks concerned the selling behavior of the sales force regarding new products. Their comment indicated that no formal sales presentation of any kind was made. Rather, in quite a number of cases, there was only a talk session lasting only a few minutes with very little evidence of any serious preparation for the call. This directly alludes to the earlier discussion regarding the capacity of the sales force to handle new items.

Signs are becoming evident now that the economic waste centering around new product development efforts are finding a sympathetic ear from corporate specialists. It was recently reported that a new company called The

Center for New Product Development, Inc. has created a new concept in product development, in that the center has developed a product package and costed the product so that any future marketer knows the direct and indirect marketing costs. The company has even gone as far as developing an advertising program. The company's executives have indicated what may be the bitter truth concerning developmental work. They have said that "most companies are organized to sell existing products, not to create new ones." They have also recognized that asking a product manager to develop, market, and infuse investment spending into a product works at odds with the very responsibility he is attempting to bear.

VENTURE GROUPS

One unique approach to the problem inherent in new product development has been created by the new products division of the Cudahy Company. They established what they call a "venture group." In essence, this group is an entrepreneural team that has direct responsibility for achieving the payout for research and development funds which are assigned to it. It has been given specific objectives and profit responsibility. In addition to this, the group has been assigned a time limitation within which it must show achievement. Because of the very fact that the group deals in high risk products and deals in speculative areas, it is essential that qualified talent be attracted to the group. They have indicated that "a venture team can be made up from as few as three or four creative people, deeply versed in the disciplines of marketing, financial, economic and consumer analysis, technical development, production and costs. The key feature is that all of the venture team must have broad backgrounds which allow them to contribute to all phases of the venture, not just their speciality." According to the group, the functions of their venture team include:

1. Top management contact
2. Constant development
3. Strategy sessions
4. Client solicitations
5. Team administration

In addition, members of the group are individually responsible for such ancillary jobs as concept development, market research programs, marketing planning, sales testing, and product administration. What has emerged from this experiment is an organization not unlike independent management consultants. As it functions, the venture group is really an internal management consulting team consisting of selected experts in various aspects of product development. This is not a unique feature in and of itself; however, its uniqueness lies in the fact that this group has been charged with an independent profit responsibility and been given a specific time horizon for development.

CONTRIBUTION OF DISCIPLINED LOGIC
TO ALLEVIATING WASTE

Marketing is also awakening to the sometimes virtue of employing operations research techniques for new product decision-making. The author is referring specifically to application of Bayesian Analysis and employment of the Critical Path Method to product planning. Bayesian Analysis is a technique that will be discussed in more depth in a later chapter. However, at this point, it is sufficient to say that it is an applied mathematical technique which utilizes probabilities in assigning the weight or likelihood of an event occurring. As an example, if the reader is crossing a crowded highway and intuitively estimates that his chances of reaching the other side unscathed are only 50–50, this in terms of Bayesian Analysis would be an expression indicating that the probability of reaching the other side unharmed is 50%. It is no different from recognizing the odds one encounters in a bet on a sporting event, such as a horse race or a football game.

One of the most concrete methods of ensuring a successful new product program is the enforcement of a discipline of logic and an establishment of priorities. The Product Improvement Decision Guide (Fig. 4) is a vehicle which can be adapted for most research and development applications. If properly administered and entered into in a spirit of venture, the Decision Guide could become the means by which risks and rewards are properly shown in perspective.

Of all of the applications of the ROI technique, capital project analysis is probably the most familiar. Exhibits 33 through 37[19] illustrate a problem involving the principles of capital project analysis as they apply to new product development.

---

[19] Exhibit 33 through 37 in this work appeared in an article written by the author entitled "Expanded Uses of the ROI Concept" in the March 1968 issue of *Financial Executive*.

FIG. 4

PRODUCT IMPROVEMENT DECISION GUIDE

MARKETING DIVISION: _____ TITLE: _____

LOCATION: _____ PROJECT NUMBER: _____ DATE: _____

I. PRODUCT DESCRIPTION

A. _____ New Product   _____ Quality Improvement

   _____ New Size   _____ Exploratory Research

   _____ New Flavor   _____ Concept Testing

B. General product description, major uses, consumer advantages and competitive advantages where applicable: _____
_____
_____
_____

C. Rationale, or justification for project proposal: _____
_____
_____
_____

D. Specific Objectives: _____
_____
_____
_____

II. URGENCY AND RISK

A. Urgency . . . . . .
___ Normal development cycle
___ Longer than normal development cycle
___ Crash program - speed essential

B. Degree of Risk . . . . . .
___ Virtually none
___ Moderate
___ Substantial

III. COMPETITION

When possible, for each known competitive or related product include brand or description, unit size and/or number of servings, package type, (carton, glass, etc.), unit retail price, estimate yearly volume, number of years on market, distribution pattern description, estimated yearly advertising or promotional expenditures; and general comments on product advantages and disadvantages: _____

_____

_____

_____

_____

IV. TECHNICAL INFORMATION

A. Manufacture of Product
1. a) Our Manufacture _____   b) Indicate Manufacturing Locations:
   c) Outside Processors _____   _____

FIG. 4 (Continued)

141

FIG. 4 (Continued)

2. Is new equipment required?   _____ Yes   _____ No

   If yes, complete below:

Incremental Investment	19___	19___	19___	19___	19___	19___	Total
1) Capital Cost							
2) Related Expense							
3) Working Capital							
T o t a l							
Depreciation							

3. Proposed Supplier of raw materials for production: _____

   Comment only if problem is anticipated: _____

4. Special manufacturing problems: _____

B. Finishing Supplies

1. Type of Container:

_____ Jar _____ Can _____ Envelope

_____ Other: _____ Specify _____

2. Attach sketch or photo of package design, if possible.

3. Comment on technical packaging requirements: _____

_____

_____

C. Product Stability

1. Shelf life in recommended packages: _____

2. Container compatability: _____

3. Other stability problems: _____

FIG. 4 (Continued)

143

FIG. 4 (Continued)

V. DISTRIBUTION

A. _____ Existing Sales Force

_____ Additional Salesmen to be hired

_____ Other

B. Warehousing and Handling Facilities: _____

_____

_____

_____

_____

C. Comments on special manufacturing, shipping, storage, handling problems, etc.: _____

_____

_____

_____

_____

VI. PROFITABILITY

A. Forecast   (Incremental Only)

	19	19	19	19	19	19	19	19	19	19	19
Net Sales											
Variable Profit											
Advertising											

Promotions							
Selling Expense							
Division Profit							
Incremental Exp.							
Net Profit							

B. Expected unusual promotion vehicles: _____
_____
_____
_____

C. Will the proposed product or process allow royalty payments?

_____ Yes _____ No

VII LIFE CYCLE

A. Estimated time for basic development _____

B. Estimated time for test marketing _____ (cum.)

C. Estimated time for national distribution _____ (cum.)

D. Estimated time for maturity* _____ (cum.)

*Softening of price structure, marginal return of marketing investment, proliferation of competition, decline of consumer preference for brand.

FIG. 4 (Continued)

145

FIG. 4 (Continued)

VIII. PROBABILITY OF SUCCESS

	Technical	Marketing
0 - 25%	_____	_____
25 - 50%	_____	_____
50 - 75%	_____	_____
75 - 100%	_____	_____

IX. Using the above projections for expenditures and income, complete the attached forms to compute the Return on Investment and Payback Period and enter the results on the line below.

_____ % R.O.I.   _____ Years Payback Period

X. APPROVALS   DATE

Marketing Division

Engineering

Financial Analysis and Planning

Manufacturing Technical Services	
President	

FIG. 4 (Continued)

CAPITAL PROJECT ANALYSIS

Assume that in 1965 a company planned to construct a small plant costing $100,000 to house a manufacturing and packaging line for a product recently developed and marketed nationally. In the next year, based on a successful marketing program, machinery and equipment costing $700,000 were to be installed. Later, based on projections of growth and consumer acceptance, an additional $200,000 in machinery and equipment were required to support the volume. In viewing the Exhibits 33 through 37, it is important to note that all of the amounts shown are incremental and may not add because of rounding. The incremental approach says, in effect, that if the product were not marketed, there would be no numbers in Exhibits 33 through 37. Exhibit 33 sets forth the basics of the problem, including a section called capital data. Note that in this section, the cost of capital is computed based on the weights of market values and the after-tax rate for the various components of capital. Based on this calculation, the cost of capital is calculated at 8.6%. This compares with a target rate of return for the new product of 14%.

The reader should remember at this stage that the original definition of cost of capital, presented earlier in the book, indicated that the cost of capital may be the aggregate cost of corporate resources or it may be considered as a target rate of return. In this case, the cost of capital, since it computes at a lower rate than the target return, should be considered as a bedrock minimum acceptable criterion which cannot be violated. Exhibit 34 sets forth the major components of an incremental profit and loss statement in much the same manner as the earlier profitability concepts were shown. Note that in this schedule there is no attempt made to total the incremental cash flow of the product since it is immaterial. It is only the timing of the cash flows which becomes material in the calculation. Exhibit 35 sets forth the manner in which working capital is computed for this new product which has come on the lne. In order to compute the requirements for maintenance of receivables, it was estimated that sales terms for the product will be on a 2/10, net 30 basis, and that monies will be collected, on an average, on the fifteenth day. There are, of course 24 15-day periods in a year of 360 days. Therefore, in the calculation the sales each year are divided by the number of periods of collection. Inventories for this purpose were based on a 30-day supply of finished goods and a two-month supply of raw materials for the product.

The total working capital is then calculated but only the increments used for purposes of the problem. Mathematically, the total of the increments should equal the total of aggregate working capital in the last period. Note also that the incremental working capital needed over the life of the product totals $2.5 million. This contrasts with an outlay for capital of $1 million.

It was this very point that the author made earlier in the book, that *frequently the requirements for incremental working capital overshadow those for project capital.*

Exhibit 36 shows the beginnings of the actual calculation. It takes the investment data from the problem and sets it forth in terms of the project capital and the incremental working capital. For purposes of the calculation, trials were made at a 10% rate and a 15% rate. Exhibit 37 takes the receipts side of the equation as they were originally shown on Exhibit 34 and discounts those at the same trial rates. These calculations show that the trial rate of 15% results in a numerical total which makes the receipts equal to the investment. This is the desirable end result of the discounted cash flow technique. Therefore, the answer to the problem is that the new products development effort with its required capital project will return 15% to the corporation.

Note that as previously shown in the first example, the $2.5 million of working capital is assumed to be returned in the year 1980, the last year of the time horizon for the project.

EXHIBIT 33   Company Alpha, Capital Project Analysis

Assume:

Product Gamma, a new product, is being considered for manufacture and distribution. P&L data is as shown:

Estimated cost of plant	$0.1 million 1965
Estimated cost of machinery and equipment	0.7 million 1966
Estimated cost of machinery and equipment	0.2 million 1969

Target return: 14%
Capital data:

	Market Value	Rate after Tax	Dollar Cost
Notes payable	$ 100,000	4%	$ 4,000
Debentures	400,000	3%	12,000
Preferred stock	200,000	5%	10,000
Net worth (capital stock)	2,500,000	10%[a]	250,000
	$3,200,000		$276,000

Cost of capital = $276,000/$3,200,000 = 8.6%

[a] Earnings/Price.

EXHIBIT 34   Product Gamma, Profit and Loss (Millions of Dollars)

Year	Sales	Variable Cost	Variable Profit	Advertising and Promotion	Direct Profit	New Plant Period Cost	Depreciation[a]	Before Taxes	Profit after Taxes	Add Depreciation	Cash Flow	7% Credit	Total
1965	$ 3.2	$2.4	$ .8	$1.4	$ (0.6)	$ 0.3	$ —	$(.09)	$(0.4)	$ —	$(0.4)	$ 0.1	$(0.3)
1966	4.4	3.2	1.2	1.4	(0.2)	0.3	0.1	(0.6)	(0.3)	0.1	(0.2)		(0.2)
1967	5.2	3.5	1.7	1.6	0.1	0.3	0.1	(0.3)	(0.2)	0.1	(0.1)		(0.1)
1968	6.1	4.1	2.0	1.1	0.9	0.3	0.1	0.5	0.3	0.1	0.4		0.4
1969	6.7	4.5	2.2	0.9	1.3	0.3	0.1	0.9	0.5	0.1	0.6		0.6
1970	7.4	5.0	2.4	1.0	1.3	0.3	0.1	0.9	0.5	0.1	0.6		0.6
1971	7.7	5.2	2.5	0.7	1.8	0.3	0.1	1.4	0.7	0.1	0.8		0.8
1972	8.0	5.4	2.6	0.7	1.9	0.3	0.1	1.5	0.8	0.1	0.9		0.9
1973	8.4	5.7	2.7	0.8	1.9	0.3	0.1	1.5	0.8	0.1	0.9		0.9
1974	8.8	6.0	2.8	0.8	2.0	0.3	—	1.7	0.8	—	0.8		0.8
1975	9.1	6.2	2.9	0.8	2.1	0.3	—	1.8	0.9	—	0.9		0.9
1976	9.5	6.5	3.0	0.9	2.1	0.3	—	1.8	0.9	—	0.9		0.9
1977	9.9	6.7	3.2	0.9	2.3	0.3	—	2.0	1.0	—	1.0		1.0
1978	10.2	7.0	3.2	0.9	2.3	0.3	—	2.0	1.0	—	1.0		1.0
1979	10.6	7.2	3.4	0.9	2.5	0.3	—	2.2	1.1	—	1.1		1.1
1980	11.0	7.5	3.5	1.0	2.5	0.3	—	2.2	1.1	—	1.1		1.1

[a] Does not add because of rounding.

EXHIBIT 35   Product Gamma, Computation of Working Capital (Millions of Dollars)

Year	Accounts Receivable		Inventories	Total Working Capital	Increment
	Sales	Divided by 24			
1965	$3.2	$0.1	$0.7	$0.8	$0.8
1966	4.4	0.2	0.8	1.0	0.2
1967	5.2	0.2	0.9	1.1	0.1
1968	6.1	0.3	1.1	1.4	0.3
1969	6.7	0.3	1.2	1.5	0.1
1970	7.4	0.3	1.3	1.6	0.1
1971	7.7	0.3	1.4	1.7	0.1
1972	8.0	0.3	1.4	1.7	—
1973	8.4	0.3	1.5	1.8	0.1
1974	8.8	0.4	1.6	2.0	0.2
1975	9.1	0.4	1.6	2.0	—
1976	9.5	0.4	1.7	2.1	0.1
1977	9.9	0.4	1.8	2.2	0.1
1978	10.2	0.4	1.8	2.2	—
1979	10.6	0.4	1.9	2.3	0.1
1980	10.0	0.5	2.0	2.5	0.2
					2.5

EXHIBIT 36 Product Gamma, Discounted Cash Flow (Investment) (Millions of Dollars)

Investment	Capital	Incremental Working Capital	Total	Trial 10%		Trial 15%	
1965	$0.1	$0.8	$0.9	0.9516	$0.9	0.9286	$0.8
1966	0.7	0.2	0.9	0.8611	0.8	0.7993	0.7
1967		0.1	0.1	0.7791	0.1	0.6879	0.1
1968		0.3	0.3	0.7050	0.2	0.5921	0.2
1969	0.2	0.1	0.3	0.6379	0.2	0.5096	0.1
1970		0.1	0.1	0.5772	0.1	0.4386	—
1971		0.1	0.1	0.5223	0.1	0.3775	—
1972		—	—	0.4726		0.3250	—
1973		0.1	0.1	0.4276	—	0.2797	—
1974		0.2	0.2	0.3869	0.1	0.2407	—
1975		—	—	0.3501		0.2072	—
1976		0.1	0.1	0.3168	—	0.1783	—
1977		0.1	0.1	0.2866	—	0.1535	—
1978		—	—	0.2593		0.1321	—
1979		0.1	0.1	0.2347	—	0.1137	—
1980		0.2	0.2	0.2124	—	0.0979	—
	$1.0	$2.5	$3.5		$2.5		$1.9

EXHIBIT 37 Product Gamma, Discounted Cash Flow (Receipts) (Millions of Dollars)

Receipts	Total	Trial 10%	Total	Trial 15%	Total
1965	$ (0.3)	0.9516	$ (0.3)	0.9286	$ (0.3)
1966	(0.2)	0.8611	(0.2)	0.7993	(0.2)
1967	(0.1)	0.7791	(0.1)	0.6879	(0.1)
1968	0.4	0.7050	0.3	0.5921	0.2
1969	0.6	0.6379	0.4	0.5096	0.3
1970	0.6	0.5772	0.3	0.4386	0.2
1971	0.8	0.5223	0.4	0.3775	0.3
1972	0.9	0.4726	0.4	0.3250	0.2
1973	0.9	0.4276	0.4	0.2797	0.2
1974	0.8	0.3869	0.3	0.2407	0.2
1975	0.9	0.3501	0.3	0.2072	0.2
1976	0.9	0.3168	0.3	0.1783	0.2
1977	1.0	0.2866	0.3	0.1535	0.2
1978	1.0	0.2593	0.3	0.1321	0.2
1979	1.1	0.2347	0.3	0.1137	0.1
1980	3.5 a	0.2124	0.7	0.0979	0.1
			$ 4.1		$ 1.9

a Includes recovery of working capital.

Difference + 1.6 = 0.

Answer — return on investment = 15%.

8

Return on Investment Applications in Lease versus Purchasing Decisions

I n an interesting article which appeared in the October 1968 issue of *Financial Executive,* George L. Marrah discussed the problem of leasing versus ownership for various equipment. One of the more interesting theses which he advanced was that leasing represents a complete departure from the traditional idea that it is essential for a capitalist business to own its property. This heritage of a restrictive business attitude is quite understandable since leasing, as a means of supplying the business with quasi capital, did not really reach fruition until after the Korean War. In the context of the subject of the article, Mr. Marrah sent a questionnaire to sixteen manufacturers who were asked to rank the advantages and disadvantages of leasing as they saw it on a scale from one to ten. Only half of the questionnaires were returned to Mr. Marrah; however, their results are extremely interesting.. The responses are shown in Exhibit 38.

One of the more obvious responses is the one which indicates that one of the primary examples of advantages of leasing in the eyes of the respondents is that it conserves working capital. This point alone hits at one of the major justifications for a leasing decision. The companies that are weak in working capital are the very companies that should be looking at leasing arrangements for supplying their equipment needs. On the contrary, a company that has all the working capital, including short-term bank credit and long-term debt financing, will not be helped by leasing arrangements. The only saving grace in leasing for a company which is strong in working capital is that it may help the company to rid itself of some of the administrative headaches involved with ownership. There are very real questions

EXHIBIT 38   Advantages and Disadvantages of Leasing—Survey of 30 Manufacturers[20]

Advantages	High	Medium	Low
Permits greater flexibility in use	5%	68%	27%
Encourages trying new equipment	37	37	26
Shifts the risk of obsolescence from user to buyer	47	37	16
Conserves working capital	53	32	15
Low cost	5	21	74
Tax advantage	5	20	75
Eliminates problem of equipment disposal	47	32	21
Preserves credit capacity	42	37	21
Avoids restrictive covenants in bank loan	32	37	31
Eliminates maintenance problems	16	42	42
Disadvantages			
High cost	70%	21%	8%
Does not build an equity	53	26	21
Tax disadvantages	5	53	42
Increases fixed obligations	68	27	5
Difficult to get improvements on leased equipment	16	37	47
Reluctance to absorb loss if equipment becomes obsolete	10	63	27
Forced to use inferior supply items in leased equipment	0	37	63
Objectionable clauses and limitations	31	47	22
Curtails freedom of the lessee in use of equipment	21	37	42
Difficult to finance improvements on leased equipment	5	47	48

[20] Exhibit 38 originally appeared in an article written by George L. Marrah in the October 1968 issue of *Financial Executive*, entitled "To Lease or Not to Lease?"

which companies must ask themselves as to whether they are willing to incur an added interest burden on capital through a leasing arrangement when their own cash is available. The answer to the question, of course, is contingent upon their own opportunity rate for alternative investments. As a general rule, however, those companies who have sufficient capital to continue their business and support its growth will rarely find justification in leasing or borrowing arrangements.

Note also in the replies that one of the main disadvantages cited by the respondents was that the equipment does not build an equity, as if there is an implication that there is something unholy in this outcome. The building of equity accomplishes nothing unless it is built with a rate of return which is greater than the alternative investment opportunity. In addition to this, in times of high inflation, it may be far more prudent for a company to engage in long-term leasing arrangements and pay back to the leasing company dollars of much cheaper value while, at the same time, conserving their own working capital and investing dollars in avenues which will help them keep current, for example, securities.

Another interesting reply from the respondents citing major disadvantages of leasing arrangements is the one in which they state that leasing increases fixed obligations. This is a belated recognition on the part of these companies that leasing arrangements are merely a substitution for debt and that a classification or nonclassification on the balance sheet or the semantic differential of lease versus ownership still does not change the basic nature of the transaction. Another interesting reply by the respondents is the lack of enthusiasm by the respondents over the tax advantages of leasing versus ownership. This is a healthy response and might tend to indicate that the respondents are in a somewhat comfortable working capital position.

In the context of discussing leasing decisions, four separate examples will be used .The examples will be as follows.

1. Lease versus purchase of a microfilm system
2. Leasing versus ownership of automobile sales fleet
3. Leasing versus ownership versus alternative leasing for computer hardware
4. Leasing versus ownership of raw materials warehouses

MICROFILM SYSTEMS

In the particular case of evaluating a lease versus purchase of a microfilm system, for purposes of the problem, it is assumed that in the sixth year

EXHIBIT 39 Lease versus Purchase

Year	Lease Cost	Less		Savings from Purchasing	After-Tax Savings	Cash Flow
		Depreciation	Maintenance			
0	Investment $6400					
1	$2580	$ 644	$ —	$1936	$ 968	$1612
2	2580	644	362	1574	787	1431
3	2580	644	362	1574	787	1431
4	2580	644	362	1574	787	1431
5	2580	644	362	1574	787	1431
6						
Sale	—	(1000)		1000	500	500
Writeoff		3200		(3200)	(1600)	1600
						$9436

of ownership the owner will be able to sell the used equipment for $1000. Exhibit 39 illustrates one method of analyzing such a situation. Note that under the purchase option, a non-cash charge of $644 would be incurred if the system were purchased. The $644 is represented by depreciation expense. At the same time, by owning the equipment, the company will forego a lease cost of $2580 annually. This creates a relative savings before tax of $1936, or a cash flow of $1612 after the non-cash charge is added back to the after-tax savings. The total of cash flows after the disposition of the equipment is $9436. Utilizing the discounted cash flow method of equating the income (relative savings) with the investment (purchase of the equipment), the rate of return, when comparing the advantages of purchasing versus the advantages of leasing, equates to 13%. This rate can then be compared with a predetermined target or with the cost of capital if it is other than the target.

SALESMEN'S AUTOS

One of the commonly recurring problems which faces multi-product companies periodically is the question of whether they should lease or own salesmen's autos. In a fairly recent study conducted for the Foundation for Management Research, the point was noted that auto fleet leasing has by now gone through three distinct periods. The report noted that the first period occurred immediately after World War II when corporate treasuries were in solid condition and the vehicles in short supply. The second period occurred in the decade after that when there was no question about the plentiful supply of vehicles but, in a contrary fashion, the money supply was tight. Since that time, or in the period after 1960, the money supply was more plentiful and the country began to enter into the longest period of prosperity in economic history. From the point of view of cash flow, corporate treasuries are in a healthy position. However, the burgeoning role of capital improvements has caused an increased commitment for those funds and, therefore, there has been a relative decline in corporate liquidity.

The conservation of company cash through leasing is said by the Foundation to be one of the very major reasons for the shift to auto fleet leasing in the period since World War II. They reason that for many companies leasing is said to be less expensive on an absolute basis than other modes of auto fleet operation because it has enabled the company to stabilize its costs. One of the ways in which the Foundation suggests that the lease versus purchase decision be made is via the vehicle of a comparative worksheet which reduces costs to an average cost per mile for ownership versus lease. The outline of such a worksheet is shown in Exhibit 40.

EXHIBIT 40   Cost Data for Fleet Economy Study

	Annual Cost Per Car		
	15,000 miles	20,000 miles	25,000 miles
Company Owned Fleet			
Fixed costs			
Depreciation			
Wash			
License and taxes			
Administration			
Anti-freeze			
Insurance			
Accident repairs			
Total fixed costs per car			
Operating expenses			
Gas at 2.20¢ per mile			
Repairs and greasing at .48¢ per mile			
Oil and oil changes at .1¢ per mile			
Tires			
Total operating expenses			
Total annual cost			
Average cost per mile			

	Average Monthly Cost Per Car		
	15,000 miles per year	20,000 miles per year	25,000 miles per year
Company Leased Fleet			
Leased fleet "finance plan"			
Rental and depreciation reserve			
Gasoline at 2.20¢ per mile			
Oil and changes at .1¢ per mile			
Repairs and greasing			
Insurance			
Tires			
Accident repairs			
Wash			
License and taxes			
Anti-freeze			
Total monthly cost per car			
Average cost per mile			

EXHIBIT 41   Lease/Ownership Evaluation for Sales Autos

Lease/Ownership Evaluation for Sales Autos (per car)	Column 1 Loan Service Payment	2 Interest portion	3 Principal Portion	4 Depreciation	5 Admin. Costs
1 Key to headings - Columns					
2					
3 Alternative I - Ownership					
4					
5 Year 1	$1027	$209	$818	$818	$34
6 2	966	147	818	818	34
7 Trade-in	1145		1145	1145	
8 Totals	$3137	$356	$2781	$2781	$68
9					
10					
11 Alternative II - Leasing	Lease				Admin. Costs
12	Payments				
13					
14					
15 Year 1	$921				$17
16 2	876				17
17 Less - Trade in	315				
18 Totals	$2112				$34
19					
20					
21 Return on Investment					
22 (Discounted cash flow)			Less		
23				Admin.	Pref. Lease
24	Cost of	Depreciation	Interest	Costs	pur purchase
25	Leasing				
26					
27 Year 0 - Invst. 2781					
28 1	$938	$818	$209	$34	(123)
29 2	893	818	147	34	(106)
30 Payment to lessor in trade-in	315				315
31 Trade-in with ownership		1145			
32 Totals		$2781			
33					
34					
35					

EXHIBIT 41

6	7	8	9	10		
Reduction in taxable inc.	Lower taxes	Cost of ownership	Present worth factor @ 7.5%	Present worth		
8+4+5	6+½	1-5-7				
$1361	$530	$531	.9302*	$494	*year end	
999	499	600	.8653	433		
		$1031		$927		
Reduction in tax'ed income	Lower taxes	Cost of leasing	Present worth factor - 7.5%	Present worth		
$938	$469	$469	.9620*	$451	*evenly during year	
893	447	446	.8949	399		
315	157	158	.8653	197		
2146	$1073	$1073		$987		
After tax profit (loss)	Add back interest	Savings from purchasing	Cash flow	Trial @ 4% factor	amount	Trial @ 10% factor	amount
$(62)	$209	$147	$966	.954	$921	.950	$917
(53)	147	94	912	.875	798	.864	788
158		158	168	.847	133	.846	131
			1145	.842	964	.846	946
			$3180		$2816		$2782

161

There are at least two other methods of evaluating the automobile fleet problem. One of these methods involves using the present worth factors for a dollar, and the other involves utilizing the discounted cash flow approach through the return on investment concept. Exhibit 41 illustrates the two other methods of analyzing the problem. Alternative I in Exhibit 41 illustrates a calculation of the present value of ownership. It is assumed for this purpose that funds to purchase the fleet will be available to the company at 7½% and that, on an average, the useful life of such vehicles is two years at which time it is common to trade in the vehicles. Because of the implication of tax factors, it is important to separate from the entire loan amortization each year that portion which is available for interest and that portion which is earmarked for repayment of principal. Thus, column 6 in Alternative I shows that in year 1 $1061 will be the expense applicable to taxes as a result of a decision to own. That amount is the result of adding together the interest, the depreciation, and the administrative costs attributable to the ownership function. On an after-tax basis, the reduction in taxable income amounts to $530. After applying the present worth factors at 7½% to the cost of ownership, which is shown in column 8 in that exhibit, the total present worth or, in effect, the present cost of ownership is $927 per vehicle. Although trade-in values are part of the problem, it is assumed in this analysis that there will be a constant reinvestment in automobiles and, therefore, any gain which may come about based on an excess of trade-in value over depreciated value will be offset by like losses. The tax consequences of any such gains, therefore, will be largely ignored for this purpose.

Alternative II in the same statement illustrates the analysis of leasing costs. The payments that are fixed by contract are shown for years 1 and 2, together with their associated administrative costs. Column 6 in Alternative II shows the reduction in taxable income attributable to leasing. The net cost of leasing, aside from present values, carries over to column 8. Note there, though, that this is in effect because of any possible losses of trade-in values. The present worth factors are applied and the present worth, or again, the present cost of leasing is fixed in the calculation. This is shown as $987. The proper comparative to that amount is the $927 shown as the present cost of ownership. In this type of analysis, it can be concluded that the present worth of the reduced cost of ownership is $60 per vehicle at any point in time or, on an average for a year, $30. If it were assumed that there are 600 vehicles in question in the sales fleet, then this would equate to an annual savings of $18,000.

The third section of Exhibit 41 shows the calculation for a rate of return evaluation for the same problem. Since, in the present value analysis, ownership was more advantageous (i.e., reduced present value cost), it should be logical at the outset to assume that there will be a positive rate of return in favor of ownership as opposed to leasing. Note that in column 1, under the rate of return calculation, in year 0 an investment of $2781 is assumed. This is the same amount shown as the total of the principal portion under Alternative I (column 3). All leasing costs will be compared to this amount. Column 1 shows the cost of leasing; matched against that will be the costs associated with ownership, such as depreciation, interest, and administrative costs. The differential in terms of relative savings or relative losses is shown in column 6 of that part of the evaluation. Since these amounts have tax implications, their net base is shown in column 7, summarized in column 9. The resultant relative cash flow, which is an addition of the depreciation and relative savings from ownership, is applied to the present value factors for the discounted cash flow technique. The trials are shown for 9% and 10%. The latter is the correct answer. Note that, after giving effect to the trade-in benefits under ownership, the cash flow under the 10% factor totals $2782, matching the original investment.

Based on these calculations, we would conclude that ownership provides a rate of return of 10% or 2.5 percentage points above the 7.5% cost of capital. Expressed in annual dollar savings, based on the present value analysis shown in Alternatives I and II, the resultant savings by virtue of ownership would amount of $18,000 per year on an after-tax basis.

DATA PROCESSING EQUIPMENT

Another critical decision problem faced by many companies quite often is whether they should lease or own data processing equipment. For purposes of our illustrative problem, assume that the Dataco Processing Equipment Corporation has submitted a sale and leaseback proposal relative to certain computer equipment currently being rented from HAL. Purchase price of the equipment involved (at rates quoted by HAL) is $547,600. Under the Dataco proposal, our company would purchase the equipment from HAL for immediate resale to Dataco and subsequent rental. The rental period would run for 48 months, the estimated technological life of the equipment.

The monthly rent currently paid to HAL for the equipment included in the Dataco proposal is approximately $15,200. This amount is made up of a base rental of $13,700 plus an estimated $1500 charge for the use of equipment in excess of 200 hours per month.

The total monthly rental payment to Dataco for the same equipment has been quoted by them, under their proposal, at $9100. This quote is based on a minimum rental period of 48 months and does not include maintenance

EXHIBIT 42   Lease versus Leasing of Selected Computer Equipment

Purchase vs. leasing of
FORM NO. 5775
6/94
Selected Comput. Equipment

(\$ 000's)

Plan I: Sale/leaseback with Dataco

		Cash Flow	Tax	Net Cash	Present Value	Disc. @
	4.62	Depr. Host	effect	Flow	Factor @ 8%	Value 1
1		\$ (129.6)	\$ 64.8	\$ (64.8)		
2		(129.6)	64.8	(64.8)		
3		(129.6)	64.8	(64.8)		
4		(129.6)	64.8	(64.8)	3.492 (cum.)	\$ (222.4)
5		(129.6)	64.8	(64.8)		
6		(129.6)	64.8	(64.8)		
7		(129.6)	64.8	(64.8)	5.395 (cum.)	(349.7)

Plan II: Continue present rental arrangement with HAL

Year					
1	\$ (182.4)	\$ 91.y	\$ (91.y)		
2	(182.4)	91.y	(91.y)		
3	(182.4)	91.y	(91.y)		
4	(182.4)	91.y	(91.y)	3.492 (cum.)	\$ (313.0)
5	(182.4)	91.y	(91.y)		
6	(182.4)	91.y	(91.y)		
7	(182.4)	91.y	(91.y)	5.395 (cum.)	(491.0)

Plan III: Purchase equipment - borrow funds at 8%, repay from depreciation

Column =	1	2	3	4	5	6	7
	Loan	Interest	Principal			After tax	Reduced
	Repayment	portion	Portion	Depreciation	maintenance	Income	taxes
Column Pay						2+4+5	6 x 50%
Year							
1	\$ 240.9	\$ 35.6	\$ 205.3	\$ 205.3	\$ 20.4	\$ 261.3	\$ 130.7
2	150.6	22.2	128.4	128.4	20.4	171.0	85.5
3	94.1	13.9	80.2	80.2	20.4	114.5	57.2
4	142.4	8.7	133.7	133.7	20.4	162.8	81.4
Total							

		IBM				Datco		
Type	Purchase Price	Monthly Rental	monthly maintenance	Monthly Cost		Monthly Rental	Monthly Maintenance	Total Cost/invest
A	$342.8	$9.0				$6.0	.5	$6.5
B	23.0	.1				.1	-	.1
C	86.3	.9				.6	.4	1.0
D	28.6	.5				.4	.Y	.6
E	110.0	3.0				1.9	.6	2.5
F	5.9	.2				.1	-	.1
Total	$547.6	$13.7	$1.5	$10.Y		$9.1	$1.7	$10.8
Annualized				$187.4				$129.6

8	9	10						
Net Cost of Equip 1 + 5 - 7	Present Value factor @8%	Present Value $						
130.6	.9Y6	$120.9						
85.5	.857	73.3						
59.3	.794	46.6						
81.4	.735	59.8						
		$299.5						

and service which HAL would continue to provide at an estimated additional cost of $1700 per month.

In addition to the above proposals, a third alternative is also available to the company. It would involve the purchasing of the equipment from HAL and maintenance of ownership for the estimated 48-month life of the equipment.

Exhibit 42 shows the essence of Plan I. Plan I involves the sale and leaseback arrangement with Dataco Corporation. All amounts in this exhibit are expressed in rounded thousands. Plan II is an evaluation of whether the company should continue their present rental agreement with HAL. In each of the evaluations, the after-tax effect of cash flow is shown in column 4, and the present worth factors for 8%, the assumed cost of capital, are shown and summarized in column 6. Note that after the end of the 48-month period, the present value cost of the Dataco arrangement is $222.4 thousand, whereas the present value, after the same time period for the arrangement with HAL, is $313 thousand. This would yield a present value cost savings of $90.6 thousand in favor of the Dataco rental plan versus the HAL rental plan. Plan III shown on Exhibit 42 shows the effect of our company purchasing and maintaining the ownership of the equipment with borrowed funds at 6.5%, to be repaid annually with funds to be provided from the depreciation of the equipment. In the earlier analysis of auto fleet leasing, the loan repayment amount should be fractioned into that portion pertaining to interest and that portion pertaining to the repayment of principal. The net cost of ownership is shown in column 8, based on the after-tax effect of the various costs. Present worth factors are then assigned and the amount shown for present worth or, in effect, the present cost at the end of the 4-year period, computes at $299.55 thousand. The evaluation of the problem as to whether to accept the Dataco rental proposal versus the company ownership of the equipment, is that the savings as a result of accepting the Dataco proposal would total $77.1 thousand, based on the cost of ownership of $299.5 thousand and the cost of rental from Dataco of $222.4 thousand.

Under the assumption that the estimated life of the equipment is 48 months, the evaluation over the period of time of the Dataco proposal as compared to the present arrangement with HAL indicates that discounting the after-tax amounts of the rental payments of the two alternatives at an 8% rate means that the present worth of the HAL rentals is $313 thousand versus a present worth of $222.4 thousand for the Dataco proposal. In effect, this says that there is a present worth savings of $90.6 thousand by the adoption of the Dataco proposal.

The evaluation of the ownership alternative shows that the after-tax present worth cost is $299.5 thousand. Listed below is a summary of the present worth costs of the three proposed alternatives, if the Dataco processing equipment has a 4-year life:

Rent from Dataco	$222.4 thousand
Purchased outright from HAL	299.5 thousand
Rent from HAL	313.0 thousand

Adoption of the Dataco sale and leaseback proposal offers the company an estimated worth savings of $77.1 thousand over the ownership alternative and $90.6 thousand advantage over continuing the present rental arrangement with HAL. The reader should note that the foregoing evaluation of the ownership alternative has not given any provision for the possible resale value to the company at the end of the equipment's useful life.

WAREHOUSING FACILITIES

Another type of problem frequently encountered in the business world is the question of whether companies should own their own warehouses or lease outside warehousing facilities. Many reasons exist which dictate that leasing of warehouses is far superior from a profit and return point of view than the company-owned alternatives. The common thread running through all of the advantages of leasing which follow is the employment of *financial leverage* in the form of use of borrowed funds, thus permitting minimum cash investments. Concurrently many investors have chosen to enter into the warehouse leasing field. The following are common financial advantages available to lessors.

1. Warehousing charges are usually based on a premium over borrowed funds. Typical charges may be 9% of cost contrasted with 6 to 6½% borrowing costs.

2. Cash leverage has a tremendous impact when mortgage financing is used. Cash down payments of the magnitude of 10 to 20% are common with the balance funded through mortgage facilities. This gives the lessor a fivefold advantage:

(a) As the owner of record, he is entitled to all tax advantages resulting from depreciation.

(b) The cash investment is minimal.

(c) As appreciation occurs, he can pocket the cash increment resulting from renegotiation of the mortgage in subsequent periods when cash income begins to decline.

EXHIBIT 43   Soy Bean Warehouse Evaluation

SOY BEAN WAREHOUSE EVALUATION

INVESTMENT #977,500 — TWENTY

		1	2	3	4	5	6	7	8	9
2	PUBLIC WAREHOUSE COSTS	179,696	179,696	179,696	179,696	179,696	179,696	179,696	179,696	179,696
4	OWN WAREHOUSE COSTS									
5	Labor	21,490	21,490	21,490	21,490	21,490	21,490	21,490	21,490	21,490
6	Depreciation	33,156	64,189	60,008	55,951	52,008	48,175	44,445	40,811	37,252
7	operating expense (1%)	14,663	14,663	14,663	14,663	14,663	14,663	14,663	14,663	14,663
8	Interest	68,425	68,425	68,425	68,425	68,425	68,425	68,425	68,425	68,425
9	Additional real									
10	estate taxes	36,250	36,250	36,250	36,250	36,250	36,250	36,250	36,250	36,250
		173,984	205,017	200,836	196,779	192,836	189,003	185,273	181,639	178,080
11	Credit: use of relinquished									
12	bean storage for finished									
13	goods	(33,600)	(33,600)	(33,600)	(33,600)	(33,600)	(33,600)	(33,600)	(33,600)	(33,600)
15	TOTAL	140,384	171,417	167,236	163,179	159,236	155,403	151,673	148,039	144,480
17	SAVINGS BEFORE F.I.T	39,312	8,279	12,460	16,517	20,460	24,293	28,023	31,657	35,216
19	LESS: F.I.T @ 52.8%	20,757	4,371	6,579	8,826	10,803	12,827	14,796	16,715	18,594
21	NET SAVINGS - FAV/(UNFAV)	18,555	3,908	5,881	7,691	9,657	11,466	13,227	14,942	16,622
30	CALCULATION OF RETURN ON INVESTMENT BASE (Excluding Interest)									
32	NET SAVINGS AFTER FEDERAL INCOME TAXES	50,852	36,204	38,178	40,093	41,954	43,763	45,523	47,239	48,919
34	ADD: DEPRECIATION	33,156	64,189	60,008	55,951	52,008	48,175	44,445	40,811	37,252
36	TOTAL	84,008	100,393	98,186	96,044	93,962	91,938	89,968	88,050	86,171

YEAR PROJECTION										
10	11	12	13	14	15	16	17	18	19	20
179,696	179,696	179,696	179,696	179,696	179,696	179,696	179,696	179,696	179,696	179,696
21,490	21,490	21,490	21,490	21,490	21,490	21,490	21,490	21,490	21,490	21,490
33,779	30,385	26,735	23,716	21,693	20,571	19,509	18,503	17,551	16,649	15,794
14,663	14,663	14,663	14,663	14,663	14,663	14,663	14,663	14,663	14,663	14,663
68,425	68,425	68,425	68,425	68,425	68,425	68,425	68,425	68,425	68,425	68,425
36,250	36,250	36,250	36,250	36,250	36,250	36,250	36,250	36,250	36,250	36,250
174,607	171,213	167,563	164,544	162,521	161,399	160,337	159,331	158,379	157,477	156,622
(33,600)	(33,600)	(33,600)	(33,600)	(33,600)	(33,600)	(33,600)	(33,600)	(33,600)	(33,600)	(33,600)
141,007	137,613	133,963	130,944	128,921	127,799	126,737	125,731	124,779	123,877	123,022
38,689	42,083	45,733	48,752	50,775	51,897	52,959	53,965	54,917	55,819	56,674
20,428	22,220	24,147	25,741	26,809	27,402	27,962	28,493	28,996	29,472	29,924
18,261	19,863	21,586	23,011	23,966	24,495	24,997	25,472	25,911	26,347	26,760
50,558	52,160	53,883	55,307	56,262	56,792	57,293	57,768	58,247	58,643	59,047
33,779	30,385	26,735	23,716	21,693	20,571	19,509	18,503	17,551	16,649	15,794
84,337	82,545	80,618	79,023	77,955	77,363	76,802	76,271	75,768	75,292	74,841

(d) Noncash expenses (depreciation) may be sufficient to produce book losses which may be applied as a tax loss against other income.

(e) Gains from sales of property are at an applicable capital gain rate (maximum of 25%).

In addition to the above, two additional advantages are available to investors who choose to enter the area of warehouse leasing. In the first instance, warehouse financing is usually accomplished throughout the medium of lease loan, rather than a formal mortgage. Although formal mortgages can be used and will permit financing up to 92% of the principal amount, lease loans permit the owner to more easily enlarge the property even though the loans are usually limited to a principal amount of 80%. This, in effect, facilitates refinancing of the investment. Many of the investors entering into warehouse leasing also choose to spin off portions of their investment to other parties—thus, recapturing a portion of their original capital and still retaining significant rates of return and control of their investment.

Assume for purposes of our example that a proposal has been made to the Alpha Company to construct a soybean storage warehouse of approximately 60,000 square feet in area at a capital cost, including materials and handling equipment, of $977,500. The proposed warehouse, which would have a capacity of 15 million pounds of soy beans, would replace existing public warehouse storage facilities, except at peak periods when some public warehouse space would be required. In addition, some current warehouse space is being used for finished goods storage. This space is not properly a charge which should be used to evaluate the costs of raw material storage unless the elimination of that space requires additional out-of-pocket costs.

Exhibits 43 through 45 set out in detail the financial information used in evaluating the feasibility of constructing the proposed warehouse. The evaluation is based on a cost of capital of 7½%. It should be noted that the assumptions contained in the study do not give effect to any residual values nor do they give any effect to any potential increases in construction costs over the time horizon of the study. Note that Exhibit 43 is actually constructed in two stages. Stage 1 is a simple comparison of the cost of public warehousing versus a cost which would be incurred if a warehouse were built and owned by the company. The object of this portion of the analysis is to show the book effect of ownership versus the use of outside warehousing facilities. The analysis covers a time span of 20 periods and, as shown in line 21 on that exhibit, savings are expressed on an after-tax basis.

While this will demonstrate the effect on the profit and loss statement of such alternative strategies, for purposes of the return on investment calculation, the inclusion of interest, as a deduction under our own warehousing

EXHIBIT 44 Soy Bean Warehouse—Return on Investment Calculation

SOY BEAN WAREHOUSE

RETURN ON INVESTMENT CALCULATION — Year	Investment	R.O.I Base	Trial @ 6%	Result	Trial @ 7%	Result	
1	977,500	84,008	.9706	81,538	.9658	81,135	
2		100,393	.9141	91,769	.9005	90,404	
3		98,186	.8608	84,519	.8396	82,437	
4		96,044	.8107	77,863	.7829	75,193	
5		93,962	.7635	71,740	.7299	68,583	
6		91,938	.7190	66,103	.6806	62,573	
7		89,968	.6772	60,926	.6346	57,094	
8		88,050	.6377	56,149	.5917	52,099	
9		86,171	.6006	51,754	.5517	47,540	
10		84,357	.5656	47,701	.5144	43,383	
11		82,545	.5327	43,972	.4796	39,589	
12		80,618	.5016	40,438	.4472	36,052	
13		79,023	.4724	37,330	.4169	32,945	
14		77,955	.4449	34,682	.3888	30,309	
15		77,363	.4190	32,415	.3625	28,044	
16		76,802	.3946	30,306	.3380	25,959	
17		76,271	.3716	28,342	.3151	24,033	
18		75,768	.3500	26,519	.2938	22,261	
19		75,292	.3296	24,816	.2739	20,622	
20		74,841	.3104	23,231	.2554	19,114	
21							
22	977,500			1,012,113		939,369	

$$R.O.I. = 6 + \frac{34613}{72744} = .5\%$$

$$R.O.I. = 6.5\%$$

EXHIBIT 45   Soy Bean Warehouse—Fiscal Depreciation

SOY BEAN WAREHOUSE

FISCAL DEPRECIATION	BUILDING DOUBLE-DECLINING- 40 % LIFE			EQUIPMENT SUM OF YEARS DIGITS 12 YEAR LIFE		
YEAR	COST	RATE	AMOUNT	COST	RATE	AMOUNT
1	795,000	2.5%	19,875	154,500	.0769	11,881
2	775,125	5.0	38,756		.1474	22,773
3	736,369		36,818		.1346	20,796
4	699,551		34,978		.1218	18,818
5	664,573		33,229		.1090	16,840
6	631,344		31,567		.0962	14,863
7	599,777		29,989		.0834	12,885
8	569,788		28,489		.0706	10,908
9	541,299		27,065		.0577	8,415
10	514,234		25,712		.0448	6,922
11	488,522		24,426		.0319	4,928
12	464,096		22,873		.0190	2,635
13	440,841		21,939		.0061	942
14	418,847		20,942			
15	397,905		19,895			
16	378,010		18,900			
17	359,110		17,955			
18	341,155		17,058			
19	324,097		16,205			
20	307,892		15,395			
21						
22						
23						
24						
25						
26						
27						
28						
29						
30						
31						
32						
33						
34						
35						
36						
37						
38						
39						
40						
41						
42						
43						
44						
45						
46						

LAND IMPROVEMENTS
DOUBLE DECLINING - 20 YR LIFE

COST	RATE	AMOUNT	TOTAL
28,000	5.0%	1,400	33,156
26,600	10.0	2,660	64,189
23,940		2,394	60,008
21,546		2,155	55,951
19,391		1,939	52,008
17,452		1,745	48,175
15,707		1,571	44,445
14,136		1,414	40,811
12,722		1,272	37,252
11,450		1,145	33,779
10,305		1,031	30,385
9,274		927	26,735
8,347		835	23,716
7,512		751	21,693
6,761		676	20,571
6,085		609	19,509
5,476		548	18,563
4,928		493	17,551
4,435		444	16,649
3,991		399	15,794

costs (line 8), necessitates a recalculation of the operating savings. For purposes of computing the return on investment, if interest is excluded as an expense from the operating statement, the net savings after federal income taxes will be stated in a manner comparable to the return on investment method. Depreciation is then added to it to produce a cash flow based on ex-interest considerations. Note, for example, that in year 2 (lines 21 and 32) the difference between the two amounts is the after-tax effect of interest which was originally included in line 8.

EXHIBIT 46   Return on Investment Case Study

Problem

Company A

Division 1	Division 2	Division 3
Product Line	Product Line	Product Line
A	C	E
B	D	

Company A is a large, decentralized food processor with a divisionalized marketing operation.

Recently the company has been perturbed because even though profits have increased steadily for the last three years, the price of the company's stock has slipped from a high of $70 per share to the current low of $53 per share.

This has hurt the company because acquisitions have customarily been made via the stock route and, in addition, financing of capital projects, usually accomplished by selling stock has had to be cut back because of the poor reception to stock offers. Instead, the company has had to resort to borrowing and high current interest rates have hurt the capital program.

You are a management consulting group called upon to analyze the company's dilemma and make recommendations.

Given

Product	Profits [a] 1964	1965	1966	Sales [a] 1964	1965	1966
A	$11	$13	$16	$110	$130	$200
B	8	8	8	20	20	20
C	15	20	25	30	0	75
D	10	15	20	30	45	50
E	5	3	1	10	5	5
	$50	$60	$70	$200	$240	$350

[a] All figures represent thousands of dollars.

EXHIBIT 47   Return on Investment Case Study (Continued)

Product	Inventories [a]			Receivables [a]			Total [a]		
	1964	1965	1966	1964	1965	1966	1964	1965	1966
A	$ 22	$ 25	$ 40	$ 11	$ 14	$ 40	$ 33	$ 39	$ 80
B	5	5	5	5	5	5	10	10	10
C	5	10	15	40	40	60	45	50	75
D	10	30	40	20	15	30	30	45	70
E	20	20	20	12	16	25	32	36	45
	$ 62	$ 90	$120	$ 88	$ 90	$160	$150	$180	$280

[a] All figures represent thousands of dollars.

1. What is the nature of the company's fundamental problem?
2. What products are in "trouble"?
3. What steps might be taken with these products to keep corporate ROI within reasonable limits?

Solution (One of Many)
 1. Return on Investment in aggregate have fallen from 33⅓% in 1964 and 1965 to 25% in 1966. It stems from the following:

Profit Margins			Turnover		
1964	1965	1966	1964	1965	1966
33⅓%	25%	20%	1.3	1.3	1.2

The main cause of the problem is shrinking profit margins.
 2. Expressed in terms of the importance of dollar contribution, Product C is the major culprit. Its margins shrink from 50% in 1964 and 1965 to 33⅓% in 1966. Had normal margins been maintained, total corporate profits in 1966 would have been $82.5 million and ROI, 29.5%. Next in importance is product A, whose margin shrunk to 8% in 1966 from a level of 10%. That margin decline cost $4 million of profit. Product E requires immediate surgery since its margin shrunk from 60% in 1965 to 20% in 1966.
 3. Refer back to Exhibit A-4 to see how the components of each product's ROI can be beneficially changed.

Exhibit 44 is a discounted cash flow calculation based on the input in Exhibit 43. This shows that the return on investment for the ownership alternative versus the use of outside warehouse facilities is 6.5%. It should be noted that this return is below the cost of capital and, therefore, places the decision as a financially marginal alternative. Exhibit 45 is simply a worksheet showing the computation of the depreciation used on line 6 of Exhibit 43.

A RETURN ON INVESTMENT CASE STUDY

Various problems and suggested solutions for these problems have been shown to the reader in all of the foregoing discussion. Nevertheless, it may still be desirable for the reader to acquaint himself with the insight which can be given to him by means of a return on investment approach to analysis. At this point, it is desirable that an open-ended problem dealing with return on investment concepts be given to the reader for his solution. Exhibits 46 and 47 set forth the problem and the requirements. A suggested solution to the problem is shown at the end of the problem.

SUMMARY

In this exposition of the return on investment concept, the author has attempted to illustrate to the reader the creative variants of the concept. It is far too easy to sit back and accept the fact that most uses of the concept have been relegated to aggregate stockholder measures or total corporate efficiency measures. Although the concept itself is not new, as indicated earlier, its variants demonstrate a vitality which permits it to be adapted to many changing business situations. At this point the reader should be challenged to expand his financial horizon to realize the implication of a return on investment measure for customer and geographic profitability studies; for the profitability studies of factories, and groups of products, even individual products. Ultimately, through the use of better data gathering and collating systems, it may also be possible to create the ultimate in personnel motivation measures, the return on investment for an individual.

9

Return on Investment Applications in Establishing Product Price, Evaluation of Marketing Areas, and Marginal Salesmen

ESTABLISHING A PRICE FOR THE PRODUCT

One of the most vexing problems in marketing comes about when the price for a product is to be acted upon. It is felt most strongly if the product is to be acted upon. It is felt most strongly if the product is new and has no real precedent in the market. An even more complex variant of this problem is when a unique product never before made, with no competition whatsoever, comes into being in the marketplace. An example of this occurred with the development of the Polaroid Camera. Normally, there are many ways in which pricing strategy may be initiated. If the product is a "me too" product, frequently the price will simply be based on competition. If it is a new product, very often the strategy involved will be a sequence which will run the gamut from skimming through penetration strategies. The fact remains, though, that establishing a price is always a difficult conceptual area.

Marketing specialists contend that pricing should have nothing to do with cost except for bid and cost-plus contracts. The essence of pricing is that it is commensurate with the competitive situation and the uniqueness of a product. Approaching the problem in the fashion that it is being presented in the following examples is not at all in conflict with the marketing specialists' point of view because what is being suggested is that, if the option is available, a product may be priced upon an ROI goal. This is not to imply that the derived price from the calculation is the only price or *the* correct price for the product. It is, at the very least, a beginning point for rationalizing the price.

In order to show an example of the method of establishing a price through ROI techniques, the author asks the reader to revert back to Exhibits 33 through 37 because the problem uses essentially the data shown in those tables.

The volume input, in terms of millions of units, for the new product which is being developed as shown in the previous example, is as follows:

1965	5.8
1966	8.0
1967	9.3
1968	10.9
1969	12.2

In addition to the above volume input, one further piece of information is required to solve the problem. The ROI goal which is expressed in terms of a minimum acceptable criteria is 14%. At this point, refer to Exhibit 34 and reason from this point in the following manner. The end product of the problem is known, that is, the return on investment required. The investment, the denominator of the equation, is also known. It is the same as that shown in Exhibit 36. What is not known at this point, in order to solve the problem, is the *return* to be applied to the investment. The return, it will be remembered, is derived from the last column in Exhibit 34. Viewing that exhibit, mentally tick off those items in the exhibit which are known compared to those which are unknown. From right to left on that statement, it can be seen that the total cash flow *is* known. This must be so since the solution to the problem (the 14% rate of return) is already established. If we know the investment and we know the rate of return, we then must know what the total cash flow is in order to satisfy that equation. Depreciation is known based on the capital infusion. New plant period costs are also known as well as advertising and promotion costs. Variable costs are known and, based on the additional data given to the problem, volume input is also derived. The *unknown*, therefore, is sales dollars. In order to compute sales dollars, it is necessary to construct the operating statement literally from the bottom up. Sales dollars would then be backed into and subsequently divided by the units of sales given above. Summarizing the explanation just given in a different fashion may be in order at this point.

In this case, everything is known but sales dollars. We know, for example, that cash flow must total $1.9 million on a discounted basis (see last column, Exhibit 37). The aim is to back into sales dollars by utilizing the known inputs of cash flow required, variable costs, marketing costs, and incremental period expenses. Dividing the backed into sales dollars by the approximate number of units produces an assumed trial selling price of 55¢ per unit. If many kinds of pack sizes are inherent in the problem, it may lend itself easily to computer simulation.

From a quantitative point of view, this is the correct solution. However, from a marketing point of view, it represents only a first step in determining if this is a reasonable price. It does at least provide a starting point and a base as mentioned earlier.

Another approach to the same problem is through a formula developed by I. Wayne Keller in his book, *Management Accounting for Profit Control*. A good summary of his formula is also contained in the research report #35 of the National Association of Accountants. The report is called "The Return on Capital as a Guide to Managerial Decisions." Mr. Keller's formula is as follows:

$$\text{Price} = \frac{\text{Cost} + (\% \text{ Return} \times \text{Fixed capital})/\text{Volume}}{1 - (\% \text{ Return} \times \% \text{ Current assets to sales})}$$

In order to illustrate the calculation of the selling price problem utilizing this formula, we might hypothesize the following situation:

Factory costs	$200,000
Administrative period costs	30,000
Field sales force expense	50,000
Advertising and promotion expense	100,000
Total cost	$380,000

Target return on investment	25%
Fixed capital	$300,000
Number of units to sell	30,000 units
Ratio of current assets to sales	20%

The above data is incorporated into the Keller equation in the tabulation:

$$\text{Selling price per Unit} = \frac{380,000 + (.25 \times 300,000/30,000)}{1 - (.25 \times .20)}$$

The price per unit computes out to $15.95. Based on the given data in the study, this price per unit for the specified number of units will generate a return on investment of 25%, the target rate.

EXHIBIT 48   District Alpha—Return on Investment[21]

Given

The chief financial officer of Company Gamma, aware that ROI techniques are used to evaluate overall performance, queries the Controller as to why such techniques could not be used for evaluating the profitability of geographic areas and customers.

The configuration of District Alpha shows:

Sales		$2,000,000
Cost of goods manufactured		1,400,000
Gross margin		$ 600,000
Less:		
Incremental district expenses		
Salaries and fringe benefits	$200,000	
Travel and entertainment	30,000	
Sales office expense	10,000	240,000
Incremental district profit (before tax)		$ 360,000
Profit after tax		$ 180,000
Assets used:		
Receivables	$200,000	
Inventories (finished goods)	$175,000	

$$\text{Return on investment} = \frac{\text{profits}}{\text{sales}} \times \frac{\text{sales}}{\text{investment}}$$

$$= \frac{\$\ 180,000}{\$2,000,000} \times \frac{\$2,000,000}{\$\ 375,000}$$

$$= \quad 9\% \quad \times \quad 5.33$$

$$= \quad 48\%$$

---

[21] Exhibit 48 and 49 originally appeared in an article written by this author in the March 1968 issue of *Financial Executive* entitled "Expanded Uses of the ROI Concept."

EVALUATION OF A GEOGRAPHIC AREA

The evaluation of a geographic area is of utmost importance in sophisticated marketing analysis. It is especially important for those manufacturers who ship liquid products to the west coast over the Rocky Mountains. This type of analysis is the key to establishing whether it is feasible to build manufacturing facilities on the west coast or to retain east or central facilities and transship. The essentials of the evaluation of a market area revolve around the isolation of the working capital employed in the market area and the purely incremental expenses or income attributable to the area. To be solved, two inputs are required—the incremental contribution and the determination of the incremental investment.

An example of an evaluation of a market area is shown in Exhibit 48. Sales reports, showing volume and product mix, can provide the sales input in the configuration shown in the exhibit. Cost records, showing the factory production mix on a variable cost basis, provide the input for cost of goods manufactured. Note that the measure here is not cost of goods sold since it is assumed that finished goods inventory policy is a corporate policy and is not incremental to the sales district nor is it controllable by that area.

Following next is a selection of incremental district expenses. Other items such as spot media, point of sale material, and advertising and display contracts for the district, might also be included if that information is relevant. In addition, national media, such as network television, could be reasonably approximated to the district based upon the technique of "Point of Origin" analysis—the district cost related to the national cost. Although it is not specifically shown in this example, any outside or leased warehousing facilities in the district which exist because sales are made in the district are also pertinent to the analysis.

EVALUATION OF A MARGINAL SALESMAN

Most of the evaluation of a salesman shown in Exhibit 49 is self-explanatory. Companies regularly receive volume and sales input on a geographic basis. It should not be too difficult to isolate the types of products sold by given salesmen in a geographic sales force. At worst, it may be assumed that a given salesman will sell the products in the same mix as the entire geographic area. Given that information or assumption and applying relevant cost data as shown in Exhibit 49, the variable or incremental profit which derives from the sale of this merchandise can be extracted. It is then simple to apply this rate to the incremental investment in the salesman. That investment consists mainly of salary, fringe benefits, and travel expenses. In the example shown in Exhibit 49 the salesman is expected to gross $100,000 in sales volume. The sales mix produces an incremental variable profit of $40,000 or, expressed as a percent of sales, 40%. The incremental costs of the salesman are as shown:

Salary	$10,000
Fringes and other	5,000
Total investment	$15,000

Because of the relevant cost approach, which was undertaken in this analysis, the break-even sales level for this marginal salesman can be established almost immediately. The period or fixed overheads applicable to this salesman total $15,000. This amount is divided by the variable profit relationship to sales (40%). This yields a break-even sales volume of $37,500. Beyond that point, every dollar of sales produces an additional 40¢ of incremental variable profit per dollar of sales. The ROI for the marginal salesmen, therefore, calculates out at: $25,000 divided by $15,000 equals 167%. This calculation is derived from the following relationships:

Gross expected volume	$100,000
Breakeven sales volume	−37,500
Resultant incremental sales	$ 62,500

In a technical sense, the above analysis was not a true return on investment calculation since all of the items used in the calculation were operating

EXHIBIT 49   Evaluation of a Marginal Salesman

Given

The salesman is expected to gross $100,000 in sales volume.
The sales mix produces an incremental variable profit of $40,000.
Incremental costs of the salesman are:

Salary	$10,000
Fringes, other	5,000
Total investment	$15,000

Break-Even sales

$$\$15,000 \div 0.40 = \$37,500$$

Every dollar of sales above the break-even point produces $.40 of incremental variable profit. The ROI for the marginal salesman is therefore:

$$\$25,000 \div \$15,000 = 167\%$$

items and were not composed of a comparison of operating items and balance sheet items. In addition, even after taking this liberty, I have chosen to state the return on investment based on the amount over and above the break-even sales volume. Another return on investment could easily be calculated based on the entire variable profit ratio relationship with the investment in the salesman. In other words, $40,000 of incremental income related to the $15,000 of investment would produce an ROI for this marginal sales-man of about 270%. I chose to take this liberty merely to illustrate the approach of logic in attempting to relate an income with an outgo regardless of its technical propriety.

CHAPTER | 10

Using Profitability Analysis in Sales Analysis and Incentive Plan Development

A strong sales analysis program is indispensable in running an efficient corporation. Effective sales analysis can reveal a great number of factors which affect the byplay between costs and profits. Such sales analysis may entail comparatives between a planned sales amount or a sales amount derived from an historical period. In any event, the sales analysis should consist of an analysis of dollars and units of volume. The output should be expressed in terms of those variances which are caused by volume variances, variances in realization rates, variances in product mix, and variances in size mix. Information about the variation of costs with volume is extremely important in profit planning. Cost/volume/profit relationships are the keystone to the arch of effective profit planning. They are instrumental in the formulation of effective marketing strategy and plans for profitability. They are an integral part of the control of the selling function by the sales manager in that these variances play a major part in affecting the outcome of inventive plan calculations. From the administrative side, the cost/volume/profit relationships enable administrative planners to help control current costs and the financial men to cost inventories.

Another area that is vitally affected by the outcome of the cost/volume/ profit relationships is the technique of pricing for marketing. Frequently, companies establish differentials in price for various sizes of product and, in addition, have bracket prices for quantity purposes. Although the author, as stated earlier in the book, is firmly committed to the fact that pricing for marketing, especially in the consumer industry, should be based upon competition in the market and not on costs, such pricing must also be realistic in the light of cost differentials between sizes of product.

REASONS FOR SALES ANALYSIS

A few years ago, the National Industrial Conference Board studied the question of sales analysis as it is practiced in a number of successful business concerns. Their conclusion from the study was that many companies report sales data on an extremely uncoordinated basis. It was felt that although firms are now beginning to review their practices, the most important aspect of this study was that the impetus for reviewing practices regarding sales reporting stemmed from one or more of the following factors:

1. Failure to give adequate sales information to lower levels of management.

2. Shortcomings with the procedures for collecting raw sales data and/or for preparing sales reports.

3. A rapid proliferation of sales information needs.

4. The availability of machine tabulating equipment and computers.

It has been said that the only requirement for making a profit is that sales dollars exceed actual costs and expenses. This, of course, is one of the burdens that we must carry as the managerial mentality becomes more and more keyed to the stock market measures of earnings per share. Behind the earnings per share measures, there is a wealth of internal changes that take place daily. Aggregates are only the end-product of a series of seemingly unrelated inputs. Each of the inputs carries a message and an implication of its own. In this first part of the chapter, we shall attempt to lay the groundwork for establishing an effective procedure for sales analysis.

USES OF SALES ANALYSES

In addition to highlighting information about the performance of given companies in the competitive marketplace, the procedure of analyzing sales also provides a great deal of data about the executive competence of the marketing leaders. Although such sales analysis is not a vital ingredient for long-range planning, it is most immediately required for short-term profit planning. The National Industrial Conference Board report referred to earlier, cited the example of an industrial company selling through company-operated and 34 franchise dealers in the United States and Canada. They use sales analysis in the following areas of management decision-making:

Sales forecasting
Product and dealer appraisal
Setting production schedules
Planning plant and manpower requirements
Determining cash requirements
Directing sales promotions
Planning new designs for its products

The reports which underlie the company's sales analysis program include:

Factory shipments to dealers (daily)
Factory orders received from dealers (daily)
Factory orders received from dealers (weekly, with comparable data for each of the preceding five weeks)
Dealer inventory (bimonthly)
Dealer sales in units and by class of trade (bimonthly)
Annual report of sales by dealer and market

Proper forecasting for purchasing requirements and the forecast of aging for accounts receivable could also be added to this list, especially in the case of consumer companies.

Although the output of the sales analysis system may vary according to the use to which the information is going to be put, the essential analysis stems from a simple 6-column worksheet presentation as shown following:

	Col. 1	Col. 2	Col. 3	Col. 4	Col. 5	Col. 6
	Actual	Plan	Difference	Actual	Plan	Difference
Item	Sales	Sales	(1–2)	Price/Rate	Price/Rate	(4–5)
A						
B						
C						
D						
E						
F						
G						
H						

EXHIBIT 50 Sales Analyses for a Typical Product (Product A)

Pack Size	Sales Units	Dollars	Average Realization Per Unit		Unadjusted Variance	Adjusted Variance
Actual 1	2,400	$20,400	8.50	Volume	$ 5,250	
Plan	1,800	15,750	8.75	Price	(600)	
Variance	600	4,650	(.25)			
Actual 2	6,000	39,000	6.50	Volume	—	
Plan	6,000	40,500	6.75	Price	$(1,500)	
Variance	—	(1,500)	(.25)			
Actual 3	3,500	20,300	5.80	Volume	$(1,680)	
Plan	3,800	21,280	5.60	Price	700	
Variance	(300)	(980)	.20			
Total actual	11,900	79,700	6.80	Volume	$ 3,570	$ 2,004
Total plan	11,600	77,530		Price	(1,400)	(1,400)
Total variance	300	2,170		Mix		1,566

The essence of the presentation above is to produce an analysis of sales dollars which will result in a quantity of change caused by pure volume variances and another quantity which could be isolated as a result of realization rate or a product/pack mix variance. The multiplication of column 3 by column 5 produces the change attributable to *volume*. The multiplication of column 1 by column 6 produces the change produced as a result of *realization rate* or *mix changes*.

The implication of the principles contained in the above worksheet representation may be followed more easily by viewing Exhibit 50. This exhibit contains an unadjusted and an adjusted volume variance. Distinction between the two lies in the summing of volume and price variances as they have been computed for individual products and the aggregate which is the result of finding the volume variation for the total of the item. The difference between the aggregate for volume and price variances and the total dollar variances for the entire classification is then isolated and considered to be, in Exhibit 50, a size mix.

SAMPLE ANALYSES

Most problems are best attacked by considering them as artichokes and peeling back individual layers hopefully revealing further insights into the nature of the problem or the solution. In this same vein, the expansion of Exhibit 50 into further problems, illustrative of the technique for determining the variables that affect sales analysis, is summarized in the grid shown. The grid covers the situations contained in Exhibits 51 through 54. Note that on the vertical scale, problem situations dealing with product mix, case mix, total volume change for multiple products, individual product volume changes are shown, although price changes, per se, are omitted.

Situation	A	B	C	D	
Product mix	Yes	Yes	No	Yes	
Case mix	No	No	Yes	Yes	
Total volume change	No	No	Yes	Yes	
Product volume change	Yes	Yes	Yes	Yes	
Price change	No	No	No	No	

EXHIBIT 51 Sample Cost/Volume/Price Analysis—Situation A

Basic data:	Plan					Actual				
	Product 1		Product 2			Product 1		Product 2		
Size	A	B	C	D	Total	A	B	C	D	Total
Pound volume	100	200	300	600	1200	300	600	100	200	1200
Pound selling price	$1	$2	$3	$4		$1	$2	$3	$4	

Product 1	Pounds	Rate	Dollars		Variance Analysis	
					Unadjusted	Adjusted
Size A						
Actual	300	$1.00	$ 300	V	$ 200	
Plan	100	1.00	100	P	–	
Variance	200	$ –	$ 200	M	–	
Size B						
Actual	600	$2.00	$ 1,200	V	$ 800	
Plan	200	2.00	400	P	–	
Variance	400	$ –	$ 800	M	–	
Total						
Actual	900	$1.67	$ 1,500	V	$ 1,000	$ 1,000 [a]
Plan	300	1.67	500	P	–	
Variance	600	$ –	$ 1,000	M	–	
Product 2						
Size C						
Actual	100	$3.00	$ 300	V	$ (600)	
Plan	300	3.00	900	P	–	
Variance	(200)	$ –	$ (600)	M	–	
Size D						
Actual	200	$4.00	$ 800	V	$(1,600)	
Plan	600	4.00	2,400	P	–	
Variance	(400)	$ –	$(1,600)	M	–	
Total						
Actual	300	$3.67	$ 1,100	V	$(2,200)	$(2,200) [b]
Plan	900	3.67	3,300	P	–	
Variance	(600)	$ –	$(2,200)	M	–	
Products 1 and 2—Total						
Actual	1,200	$2.167	$ 2,600	V	$(1,200)	$ –
Plan	1,200	3.167	3,800	P	–	–
Variance	–	($1.00)	$(1,200)	M	–	(1,200)
						$(1,200)

[a] 600 × $1.67.
[b] (600) × $3.67.

EXHIBIT 52 Sample Cost/Volume/Price Analysis—Situation B

Basic data:		Plan					Actual			
	Product 1		Product 2			Product 1		Product 2		
Size	A	B	C	D	Total	A	B	C	D	Total
Pound volume	200	200	400	400	1200	400	400	200	200	1200
Pound selling price	$1	$2	$3	$4		$1	$2	$3	$4	

Product 1	Pounds	Rate	Dollars		Variance Analysis		
						Unadjusted	Adjusted
Size A							
Actual	400	$1.00	$ 400	V		$ 200	
Plan	200	1.00	200	P		—	
Variance	200	$ —	$ 200	M		—	
Size B							
Actual	400	$2.00	$ 800	V		$ 400	
Plan	200	2.00	400	P		—	
Variance	200	$ —	$ 400	M		—	
Total							
Actual	800	$1.50	$ 1,200	V		$ 600	$ 600 [a]
Plan	400	1.50	600	P		—	
Variance	400	$ —	$ 600	M		—	
							$ 600
Product 2							
Size C							
Actual	200	$3.00	$ 600	V		$ (600)	
Plan	400	3.00	1,200	P		—	
Variance	(200)	$ —	$ (600)	M		—	
Size D							
Actual	200	$4.00	$ 800	V		$ (800)	
Plan	400	4.00	1,600	P		—	
Variance	(200)	$ —	$ (800)	M		—	
Total							
Actual	400	$3.50	$ 1,400	V		$(1,400)	$(1,400) [b]
Plan	800	3.50	2,800	P		—	—
Variance	(400)	$ —	$ 1,400	M		—	—
							$(1,400)
Products 1 and 2—Total							
Actual	1,200	$2.17	$ 2,600	V		$ (800)	$ —
Plan	1,200	2.85	3,400	P		—	—
Variance	—	$ (.68)	$(1,200)	M		—	(800)
							$ (800)

[a] 400 × $1.50.
[b] (400) × $3.50.

EXHIBIT 53   Sample Cost/Volume/Price Analysis—Situation C

Basic data:	Plan					Actual				
	Product 1		Product 2			Product 1		Product 2		
Size	A	B	C	D	Total	A	B	C	D	Total
Pound volume	300	300	300	100	1000	150	150	100	100	500
Pound selling price	$1	$2	$3	$4		$1	$2	$3	$4	

Product 1	Pounds	Rate	Dollars		Variance Analysis	
					Unadjusted	Adjusted
Size A						
Actual	150	$1.00	$ 150	V	$ (150)	
Plan	300	1.00	300	P	–	
Variance	(150)	$ –	$ (150)	M	–	
Size B						
Actual	150	$2.00	$ 300	V	$ (300)	
Plan	300	2.00	600	P	–	
Variance	(150)	$ –	$ (300)	M	–	
Total						
Actual	300	$1.50	$ 450	V	$ (450)	$ (450)a
Plan	600	1.50	900	P	–	
Variance	(300)	$ –	$ (450)	M	–	
						$ (450)
Product 2						
Size C						
Actual	100	$3.00	$ 300	V	$ (600)	
Plan	300	3.00	900	P	–	
Variance	(200)	$ –	$ (600)	M	–	
Size D						
Actual	100	$4.00	$ 400	V	–	
Plan	100	4.00	400	P	–	
Variance	–	$ –	$ –	M	–	
Total						
Actual	200	$3.50	$ 700	V	$ (600)	$ (650)b
Plan	400	3.25	1,300	P	–	–
Variance	(200)	$ .25	$ (600)	M	–	50
						$ 600
Products 1 and 2—Total						
Actual	500	$2.30	$ 1,150	V	$(1,050)	$(1,100)c
Plan	1,000	2.20	2,200	P	–	–
Variance	(500)	$ .10	$(1,050)	M	–	50
						$(1,050)

a (300) × $1.50.
b (200) × $3.25.
c (500) × $2.20.

EXHIBIT 54   Sample Cost/Volume/Price Analysis—Situation D

Basic data:	Plan					Actual				
	Product 1		Product 2			Product 1		Product 2		
Size	A	B	C	D	Total	A	B	C	D	Total
Pound volume	100	200	300	400	1000	200	100	600	800	1700
Pound selling price	$1	$2	$3	$4		$1	$2	$3	$4	

Product 1	Pounds	Rate	Dollars		Variance Analysis	
					Unadjusted	Adjusted
Size A						
Actual	200	$1.00	$ 200	V	$ 100	
Plan	100	1.00	100	P	–	
Variance	100	$ –	$ 100	M	–	
Size B						
Actual	100	$2.00	$ 200	V	$ (200)	
Plan	200	2.00	400	P	–	
Variance	(100)	$ –	$ (200)	M	–	
Total						
Actual	300	$1.33	$ 400	V	$ (100)	$ –
Plan	300	1.67	500	P	–	–
Variance	–	$ (.34)	$ (100)	M	–	(100)
						$ (100)

Product 2						
Size C						
Actual	600	$3.00	$ 1,800	V	$ 900	
Plan	300	3.00	900	P	–	
Variance	300	$ –	$ 900	M	–	
Size D						
Actual	800	$4.00	$ 3,200	V	$ 1,600	
Plan	400	4.00	1,600	P	–	
Variance	400	$ –	$ 1,600	M	–	
Total						
Actual	1,400	$3.571	$ 5,000	V	$ 2,500	$ 2,500 [a]
Plan	700	3.571	2,500	P	–	–
Variance	700	$ –	$ 2,500	M	–	–
						$ 2,500

Products 1 and 2—Total						
Actual	1,700	$3.176	$ 5,400	V	$ 2,400	$ 2,100 [b]
Plan	1,000	3.00	3,000	P	–	–
Variance	700	$ .176	$ 2,400	M	–	300
						$ 2,400

[a] 700 × $3.571.
[b] 700 × $3.00.

A fine example of a sophisticated approach to the problem of sales analysis is shown in the summary computer program for planning (Exhibit 55) which was laid out by the systems area of a large food processor. Notice that it calls for, in phase I, a profit and loss statement which is to be laid out by case size and further, in phase II, that volume and rate mix analyses are to be produced quarterly with appropriate comparatives. A plan for volume rate and case-mix analysis is shown in Exhibit 56.

The end-product of all this analysis can be varied as indicated earlier. One such information system which is, in essence, not purely an analysis in terms of variance derivation, but rather an analysis in terms of performance variation was shown quite well in an article called "Market Mix; the Key to Profitability" by Clarence J. Ostalkiewicz.[22] His exhibits, which are self-explanatory (see Exhibits 57 through 60), are interesting because of their reliance on the margin contribution percentage. (The author believes that this is related to the concept of direct profit outlined earlier.)

INCENTIVE PLANS

Incentive plans are rarely, if ever, designed to offer true incentives. Salesmen are frequently paid for mediocre performances and, in addition, usually not paid well. Incentives as they are traditionally calculated are mainly based on volume achievements with little consideration for the qualitative factors that should be an integral part of a salesman's evaluation.

QUALITATIVE ATTRIBUTES

If the man is truly something more than an order taker, then he represents an image of service, quality, dependability, and integrity that is priceless in value. In order to accomplish a proper representation for the firm, the salesman must exhibit certain attributes that can be generally grouped into five major categories:

Knowledge
Skills
Attitudes
Work habits
Personal

---

[22] Exhibits 57 through 60 originally appeared in an article written by Clarence J. Ostalkiewicz in the January 1969 issue of *Management Accounting* entitled, "Marketing Mix; the Key to Profitability."

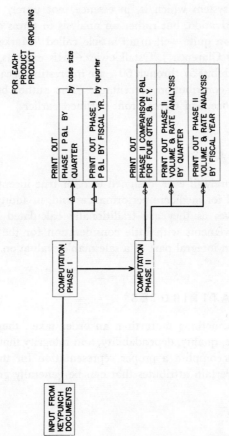

EXHIBIT 55 Computer Program for Planning

FOR EACH:
PRODUCT
PRODUCT GROUPING

INPUT FROM
KEYPUNCH
DOCUMENTS

COMPUTATION
PHASE I

PRINT OUT
PHASE I P&L BY
QUARTER   by case size

PRINT OUT PHASE I
P & L BY FISCAL YR.   by quarter

COMPUTATION
PHASE II

PRINT OUT
PHASE II COMPARISON P&L
FOR FOUR QTRS. & F.Y.

PRINT OUT PHASE II
VOLUME & RATE ANALYSIS
BY QUARTER

PRINT OUT PHASE II
VOLUME & RATE ANALYSIS
BY FISCAL YEAR

⊙ OPTION FOR PRINT-OUT

△ OPTION TO ONLY RUN
PARTICULAR PRODUCT
WHEN CHANGES OCCUR

EXHIBIT 56   Volume Rate and Case-Mix Analysis

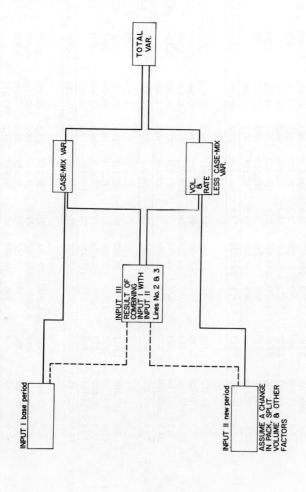

TOTAL VAR.

CASE-MIX VAR

VOL. & RATE LESS CASE-MIX VAR.

INPUT III
RESULT OF COMBINING INPUT I WITH INPUT II
Lines No. 2 & 3

INPUT I base period

INPUT II new period

ASSUME A CHANGE IN PACK, SPLIT VOLUME & OTHER FACTORS

195

EXHIBIT 57   Analysis of Margin Contribution

Division I	Price Deviation (%)	Billings	Returns and Allowances	Payment Discounts	Net Sales	Mix (%)	Standard Cost	Margin (%)	Margin	Direct Selling Expenses	Freight Out	Gross Margin Contribution	Margin Contribution (%)
Product Line A													
Distributor	13.3	296,165	2,796	5,332	288,037	38.7	204,219	29.1	83,818	14,402	2,940	66,476	23.1
Jobber	4.6	39,080	420	702	37,958	5.1	24,597	35.2	13,361	1,898	370	11,093	29.2
House account	17.2	87,451	1,032	1,571	84,848	11.4	63,891	24.7	20,957			20,957	24.7
Manufacturer	22.1	249,966	2,841	4,490	242,635	32.6	196,049	19.2	46,586	7,279	360	39,307	16.2
Retailer	2.6	33,476	122	606	32,748	4.4	20,369	37.8	12,379	2,292		9,727	29.7
Government	32.1	59,128	1,074	1,074	58,054	7.8	52,191	10.1	5,863			5,863	10.1
Total Product Line A	17.6	765,268	7,211	13,775	744,282	34.8	561,316	24.6	182,964	25,871	3,670	153,423	20.6
Product Line B													
Jobber	3.5	98,417	1,147	1,720	95,550	15.3	57,617	39.7	37,933	4,775	1,911	31,247	32.7
Distributor	12.2	270,808	3,155	4,733	262,920	42.1	170,372	35.2	92,548	13,146	5,258	74,144	28.2
Manufacturer	22.3	190,402	2,218	3,327	184,857	29.6	139,013	24.8	45,844	5,546		40,298	21.8
Retailer	2.2	50,174	585	877	48,712	7.8	28,204	42.1	20,508	2,436	1,461	16,611	34.1
Government	29.8	33,449	390	585	32,474	5.2	29,162	10.2	3,312			3,312	10.2
Total Product Line B	15.6	643,250	7,495	11,242	624,513	29.2	424,368	32.0	200,145	25,903	8,630	165,612	26.4
Product Line C													
Jobber	5.1	89,885	1,047	1,571	87,267	20.3	60,127	31.1	27,140	4,363	1,745	21,032	24.1
Manufacturer	21.8	156,745	1,826	2,739	152,180	35.4	122,201	19.7	29,979	4,565	1,818	25,414	16.7
Consumer	1.1	62,432	727	1,091	60,614	14.1	38,672	36.2	21,942	6,061		14,063	23.2
Government	32.4	133,721	1,558	2,337	129,826	30.2	117,103	9.8	12,723			12,723	9.8
Total Product Line C	25.4	442,783	5,158	7,738	429,887	20.1	338,103	21.4	91,784	14,989	3,563	73,232	17.0
Product Line D													
Distributor	6.7	79,860	930	1,396	77,534	22.8	59,314	23.5	18,220	3,877	1,550	12,793	16.5
Manufacturer	22.4	156,217	1,820	2,730	151,667	44.6	128,614	15.2	23,053	4,550	3,033	15,470	10.2
Retailer	3.4	43,432	506	759	42,167	12.4	31,157	26.1	11,010	2,952	1,265	6,793	16.1
House account	17.0	70,752	824	1,236	68,692	20.2	56,877	17.2	11,815			11,815	17.2
Total Product Line D	15.3	350,261	4,080	6,121	340,060	15.9	275,962	18.8	64,098	11,379	5,848	46,871	13.8
Total Division I	18.4	2,201,562	23,944	38,876	2,138,742	37.6	1,599,749	25.2	538,991	78,142	21,711	439,138	20.5

EXHIBIT 58   Margin Contribution: Analysis of Markets by Product

Division I	Quantity	Price Deviation (%)	Standard Sales	Billings	Credit Allowances	Sales	Cost of Sales	Margin (%)
Product Line A								
Market-Distributor								
Fargows	52,857	10.0	87,311	78,493	609	77,884	52,188	33.0
Widgets	27,082	9.2	37,712	34,243	390	33,853	21,840	35.5
Gerbets	15,473	20.4	33,266	26,480	176	26,304	23,472	10.8
Kofets	36,043	19.7	62,699	50,348	608	49,750	38,467	22.7
Guffikes	23,612	12.1	45,825	40,280	375	39,905	23,622	40.8
Spordts	31,429	11.2	74,686	66,321	632	65,683	44,630	32.1
Total distributor	186,496	13.3	341,499	296,165	2,796	293,369	204,219	31.4

EXHIBIT 59   Detail Audit Rail Analysis of Markets by Product

Division I	Customer Number	Invoice Number	Standard Price	Billing Price	Standard Cost	Quantity	Total Billing	Commission
Product Line A								
Market-Distributor								
Fargow	06A1792	C13947	1.6667	1.5000	.9873	4,941	7,412.58	370.63
Fargow	08A9437	C14282	1.6667	1.4225	.9873	10,278	14,623.14	731.15
Fargow	06A8267	C14353	1.6667	1.5000	.9873	2,308	3,462.00	173.10
Fargow	09A4218	C14372	1.6667	1.5000	.9873	3,215	4,822.50	241.13
Fargow	12A6172	C14401	1.6667	1.5000	.9873	4,432	6,648.00	332.40
Fargow	14A1792	C14428	1.6667	1.5000	.9873	2,100	3,150.00	157.50
Fargow	06A4829	C14503	1.6667	1.5000	.9873	5,040	7,560.00	378.00
Fargow	02A3246	C14741	1.6667	1.5000	.9873	8,450	12,675.00	633.75
Fargow	08A8124	C14764	1.6667	1.5000	.9873	7,145	10,717.50	535.89
Fargow	12A3231	C14847	1.6667	1.5000	.9873	1,748	2,622.00	131.10
Fargow	10A6282	C14898	1.6667	1.5000	.9873	3,200	4,800.00	240.00
Total Fargow			1.6667	1.4850	.9873	52,857	78,492.64	3,924.65

EXHIBIT 60   Customer Sales Analysis

	Month			Year to date		
	Last Year	This Year	Margin (%)	Last Year	This Year	Margin (%)	Quota
Salesman C. Smith							
A.B.C. Company							
Product Line A	5,456	6,423	24.7	20,462	22,481	24.1	24,000
Product Line B	3,081			32,470	13,070	33.7	30,000
Product Line D	4,720	7,220	32.9	46,028	52,468	17.7	48,000
Total	13,257	13,643	29.8	98,960	88,019	23.2	92,000
B.C.D. Company							
Product Line C	13,461	12,620	22.0	42,742	39,471	22.1	45,000
Product Line D	8,420			32,616	14,620	15.6	36,000
Total	21,881	12,620	22.0	75,358	54,091	20.1	81,000
Total Salesman							
Product Line A	66,723	74,832	22.9	283,172	297,821	23.1	301,000
Product Line B	36,473	22,746	32.8	152,782	121,718	32.7	160,000
Product Line C	44,167	51,436	23.9	167,342	184,620	24.1	175,000
Product Line D	47,347	38,662	16.8	201,428	172,234	16.5	220,000
Total	194,710	187,676	23.7	804,724	776,393	23.9	856,000

199

Subgroupings exist within each of the major categories as follows.

A. *Knowledge*

1. Promotion. The salesman's awareness of company policy regarding timing, offers to both the trade and consumers, type, timing, and media for advertising support, specific goals or quotas under the promotion policy.

2. Performance. In order to present the product in its best light, the salesman must be completely knowledgeable about its price, its terms, the bracket pricing for the product which may assist quantity decisions on the part of the customer, and also whatever guarantees or warranties lie behind the product.

3. Strategy. All of marketing efforts are a series of primary and secondary sales efforts. The expert salesman should have a coordinated program to follow up initial contacts with specific selling presentations.

4. Marketing. It is the expert in his field who knows his customer as it is with a victor in a contest who knows his enemy. Customers have varying degrees of importance in different markets. The challenge before the salesman is to capitalize on each customer's importance within the segment of the market he is working with. In addition to the factors regarding the importance of individual customers, a salesman should also be knowledgeable about social and economic conditions on a national scale and within the specific market he is serving.

5. Competition. No expert representative can be ignorant of the factors of competition and the attributes of competing products. He should be fully aware of their prices, their trade terms, and any specific deals or other types of promotions which may be applicable to their product.

B. *Skills*

1. Selling. The creative approach to selling might include a series of presentations, preplanned methods of overcoming objections, and an adequate supply of live samples.

2. Creativity. Ideas are priceless. The merchandising ability of the salesman, coupled with his creativity and ideas, are a future performance characteristic that should be taken into consideration in the construction of any incentive plan.

3. Planning. As distinct from organization, planning, in this vein, intends to consider any special coverages which have been arranged by the salesman and, in addition, the degree to which he plans each call.

4. Organization. In this sense, organization pertains to root planning and if applicable, merchandise stocked in the salesman's vehicle, any point of sale material or sales kit, or customer presentations.

C. *Attitudes*

1. Enthusiasm. In order to win, one must want to win and a winner

will motivate others by his own desire to achieve success. Once, when he gave some special advice, Bernard Baruch said that it is no secret to making money—if that is what you really want to do. Success in the same sense is contagious.

2. Ambition. As opposed to motivation, the successful salesman will have a personal desire to get ahead and, in order to achieve success, will willingly accept increased responsibility.

3. Positive. In terms of expressing an attitude, the positive salesman will appear confident and convincing, because this is the approach that is so important to gaining a customer's goodwill and commitment.

4. Initiative. It is quite often necessary for a salesman to act as an independent agent and take necessary action on his own part. This is an extremely important attribute and can greatly benefit the company because innovation is the mark of careful personnel selection.

D. *Work Habits*

1. Drive. The word vigorous has many connotations. However, in the world of selling, a successful representative who executes his own actions in a vigorous manner is far more likely to be the successful salesman.

2. Punctual. The sense of responsibility for giving a full day's work in return for salaries and wages is a recognition of a mature individual with responsibility.

3. Maintenance of Company Car. Just as the salesman in a personal sense represents a company, so also does a company-owned automobile.

E. *Personal*

1. Appearance. The essence of this item is so self-evident that it does not bear expansion.

The importance of all of the above discussion concerning personal attributes is that these should all be an integral part of incentive plan evaluation. Later in the discussion, a suggested method of incorporating this into such a creative plan will be shown.

THE CONTROLLER'S ROLE IN INCENTIVE PLANNING

The area of sales incentive planning is an excellent area for your controller to constructively suggest changes which may be incorporated. Based on profitability concepts, it would be a relatively simple task for the controller to demonstrate to the sales manager the optimum sales mix; perhaps suggest the playing down of an item easy to sell in favor of a more profitable, but more challenging, item to sell.

In this, we must assume that the controller has marketing sense. Obviously the most absurd application of logic is the proposal to sell the most profitable product which may also be the least desirable in the eyes of the consumer. As indicated earlier in the discussion, most incentive plans revolve around increases in sales volume. They do not encourage any awareness of how important the product mix is—of how important it is to sell products in certain proportions to one another. As a result, the individual salesman is strongly tempted to sell what is easiest for him to sell, even though what is easiest to sell may return the least profit.

The challenge in creating an incentive plan that incorporates qualitative as well as quantitative incentives is to make it dependent on profitability concepts not one some vague terminology about a product's "profit."

CREATIVE APPROACHES TO INCENTIVE PLANNING

The plan which will evolve will have as its base a "normative incentive amount" which will constitute 100% achievement of the plan. Performance beyond the plan will provide for additional monies in proportional to *incremental profitability*. Achievement of the planned incentive is dependent upon the concurrent meeting of qualitative and quantitative goals. In all the examples shown following, a single product situation is assumed. Multiple products would lend themselves easily to a data processing program.

QUALITATIVE FACTORS

For purposes of this illustration, it will be assumed that the "normative incentive amount" will total 15% of a salesman's salary. Thus a salesman earning $7000 annually can realize $1050 additional if all plan qualitative and quantitative factors are achieved. It will be further assumed that the annual evaluation for the salesman should constitute the measure·of qualitative performance. Such qualitative evaluation will constitute authority for granting up to 60% of the aggregate "normative incentive amount." A salesman, therefore, who achieves the highest qualitative grades, would be assured of earning at least $630 irrespective of profitability performance.

An example of a qualitative evaluation format is shown in Exhibit 61. Note that such a qualitative plan covers the salesmen only as individuals within the context of region or district goals. The exhibit is largely self-explanatory and the following are suggested criteria relative to the 60% ($630) aggregate incentive payout for qualitative factors:

Score	Rating	Incentive Payout %
236-241	Excellent	100%
222-235	Very good	90%
207-221	Good	80%
188-206	Fair	70%
168-205	Marginal	60%
0-167	Inadequate	0%

QUANTITATIVE FACTORS

The *quantitative* aspect of the plan gives effect to three variables:

> Volume attainment
> Product mix adjustments
> Product profitability characteristics

Assume for illustrative purposes, that Company Alpha is a manufacturer of a high-priced line of detergents which are packaged in 3 sizes—3 ounces, 9 ounces, and 15 ounces. The product profit plan envisions sales revenues of $49 million with offsetting direct expenses of $40 million. The resulting direct profit is $9 million.

The essence of the plan appreciates that profitability can be achieved in either of two ways:

1. Increase in dollar revenues
2. Decrease in controllable expenses

Exhibit 62 illustrates the construction of a grid based on profitability indices. Note, based upon *plan* expectations, that 100% attainment is shown for $49 million of revenues and $9 million of "expenses." The vertical expense column (II) is that portion of the $40 million direct expense total which is controllable by the field sales force. This recognizes that the field sales force has a certain degree of persuasive power over the headquarters marketing staff, relative to spot allowances, arrangements to meet competition, or requests for additional spot media advertising.

EXHIBIT 61   Salesman Evaluation

SALESMAN EVALUATION   SUPERVISORY EVALUATION

SALESMAN

REGION   DISTRICT   CLASSIFICATION & NUMBER   DIVISION

TERRITORY

EVALUATIONS

		By RATER DATE	By REVIEWER DATE	By INDORSER DATE
AVERAGED SUMMARY PERFORMANCES				
236–241 222–235	Excellent Very Good			
207–221	Good			
188–206	Fair			
168–205	Marginal			
0–167	Inadequate			
	TOTALS	COMPOSITE ⬆		⬇ SCORE

SALESMAN'S PROMOTABLE POTENTIAL

DEFINITE	**A**	**B**
POSSIBLE	**C**	**D**
DOUBTFUL	**E**	**F**

PERSONAL QUALITIES –

1 KNOWLEDGE

EVALUATION BY RATER				EVALUATION BY INDORSER
	PROMOTION	(TIMING, CONSUMER OR TRADE OFFER, ADVERTISING SUPPORT, QUOTAS)		
	PRODUCT	(PRICES, TERMS, BRACKETS, PRODUCT GUARANTEE)		
	STRATEGY	(PRIMARY/SECONDARY SALES EFFORT)		

MARKET (CUSTOMER IMPORTANCE, SOCIO/ECONOMIC CONDITIONS)

COMPETITION (PRICES, TERMS, DEALS)

2 SKILLS

SELLING (PRESENTATIONS, OVERCOMING OBJECTIONS, LIVE SAMPLES)

CREATIVITY (IDEAS, MERCHANDISING ABILITY)

PLANNING (SPECIAL COVERAGE, PLANNING EACH CALL)

ORGANIZATION (ROUTE PLANNING, SALES BAG, P.O.S., CAR STOCK)

3 ATTITUDES

ENTHUSIASM (MOTIVATES OTHERS BY HIS DESIRE)

AMBITION (DESIRE TO GET AHEAD, ACCEPTS RESPONSIBILITY)

POSITIVE (CONFIDENT, CONVINCING)

INITIATIVE (TAKES NECESSARY ACTION ON HIS OWN)

4 WORK HABITS

DRIVE (EXECUTES ACTIONS VIGOROUSLY)

PUNCTUAL (FULL DAY'S WORK)

MAINTENANCE OF COMPANY CAR (SERVICED, CLEAN)

5 PERSONAL

APPEARANCE (CLOTHES, SHOES, HAIR, FINGERNAILS)

TOTALS

DAILY SALES REPORT SUMMARY-PER SALES CYCLE

PART I AVERAGED TOTAL

PERCENTAGE OF OBJECTIVES ACHIEVED

GRAND TOTALS

EXHIBIT 62   Sales Incentive Formula

$$\frac{(A^1 - Z)^x}{(A - Z)} \times \frac{(B)^y}{(B^1)} \times C =$$

A^1 = Actual revenues
A = Budgeted revenues
B^1 = Actual expenses (promotion and advertising)
B = Budgeted expenses (promotion and advertising)
C = Normal incentive payment
XYZ = Coefficients

I. Revenue

Revenue	$ 46	$ 47	$ 48	$ 49	$ 50	$ 51	$ 52
Direct profit	$ 6	$ 7	$ 8	$ 9	$ 10	$ 11	$ 12
Profit index	130	140	150	160	170	180	190

II. Controllable expenses [a]

$ 6	99	135	178	225	277	335	401
$ 7	73	99	130	165	203	246	294
$ 8	56	76	100	127	156	189	226
$ 9	44	60	79	100	123	149	178
$10	36	49	64	81	100	121	144
$11	29	40	53	67	82	100	119
$12	25	34	44	56	67	83	100

[a] In millions.

The principle is that profit derived from a reduction in controllable expenses is more desirable than an additional million dollars in revenue. This can be seen through the relationships with the indices. As an example, if the reader will spot in the vertical column sales revenues of $49 million with controllable expenses of $9 million, this shows that 100% of attainment is possible. This is also the same amount shown on the profit plan. If the salesmen can sell an additional $1 million of the product, with the same controllable expenses held at a level of $9 million, he can achieve 123% of the normative incentive. The important point to notice is that, if the salesman can achieve the planned sales of $49 million with a reduction of $1 million of controllable expenses, he will achieve 127% of the normative incentive, proportionately higher than if he sold additional product. The reasoning behind this principle is simply that an increment in sales· dollars must compensate for various percentages of expenses which will culminate ultimately in an effect on profits, whereas a reduction of expenditures will have an immediate affect on profits.

The entire grid was constructed based upon the sales incentive formula shown in Exhibit 62. The X-Y-Z coefficients are there merely to permit the